Space Needle Corporation

SEATTLE

A FUN-FILLED, FACT-PACKED TRAVEL & ACTIVITY BOOK

by Donna Bergman

Donna Bergman

John Muir Publications

Santa Fe, New Mexico

Northwest Trek

John Muir Publications,
P.O. Box 613, Santa Fe, NM 87504

Printed in the United States of America
First edition. First printing September 1996

Library of Congress Cataloging-in-Publication Data
Kids Go! Seattle / Donna Bergman. — 1st ed.
p. cm.
Summary: Provides information on landmarks, museums, parks, sports, activities, entertainment, restaurants, and more things to see and do in Seattle.
Includes index.
ISBN 1-56261-307-3 (pbk.)
1. Seattle Region (Wash.)—Guidebooks—Juvenile literature. 2. Family recreation—Washington (State)—Seattle Region—Guidebooks—Juvenile literature.
[1. Seattle (Wash.)—Guides.] I. Title
F899.s43B49 1996
917.97'7720443—dc20 96-2386
CIP
AC

Editors Rob Crisell, Peggy Schaefer, Lizann Flatt
Production Nikki Rooker
Graphics Joanne Jakub
Typesetting Leslie Anderson, Nikki Rooker
Activities Rob Crisell
Cover Design Caroline Van Remortel
Cover Photo Leo de Wys Inc./de Wys/TPL/Jacobs
Back Cover Photo Northwest Trek
Illustrations Stacy Venturi-Pickett
Maps Susan Harrison
Printer Burton & Mayer

Distributed to the book trade by
Publishers Group West
Emeryville, California

CONTENTS

Northwest Trek

Seattle Aquarium/ Leo J. Shaw

COLOR THE ROUTE FROM YOUR HOMETOWN TO SEATTLE

If you're flying, color the states you'll fly over. If you're driving, color the states you'll drive through. If you live in Seattle or Washington, color the states you have traveled to.

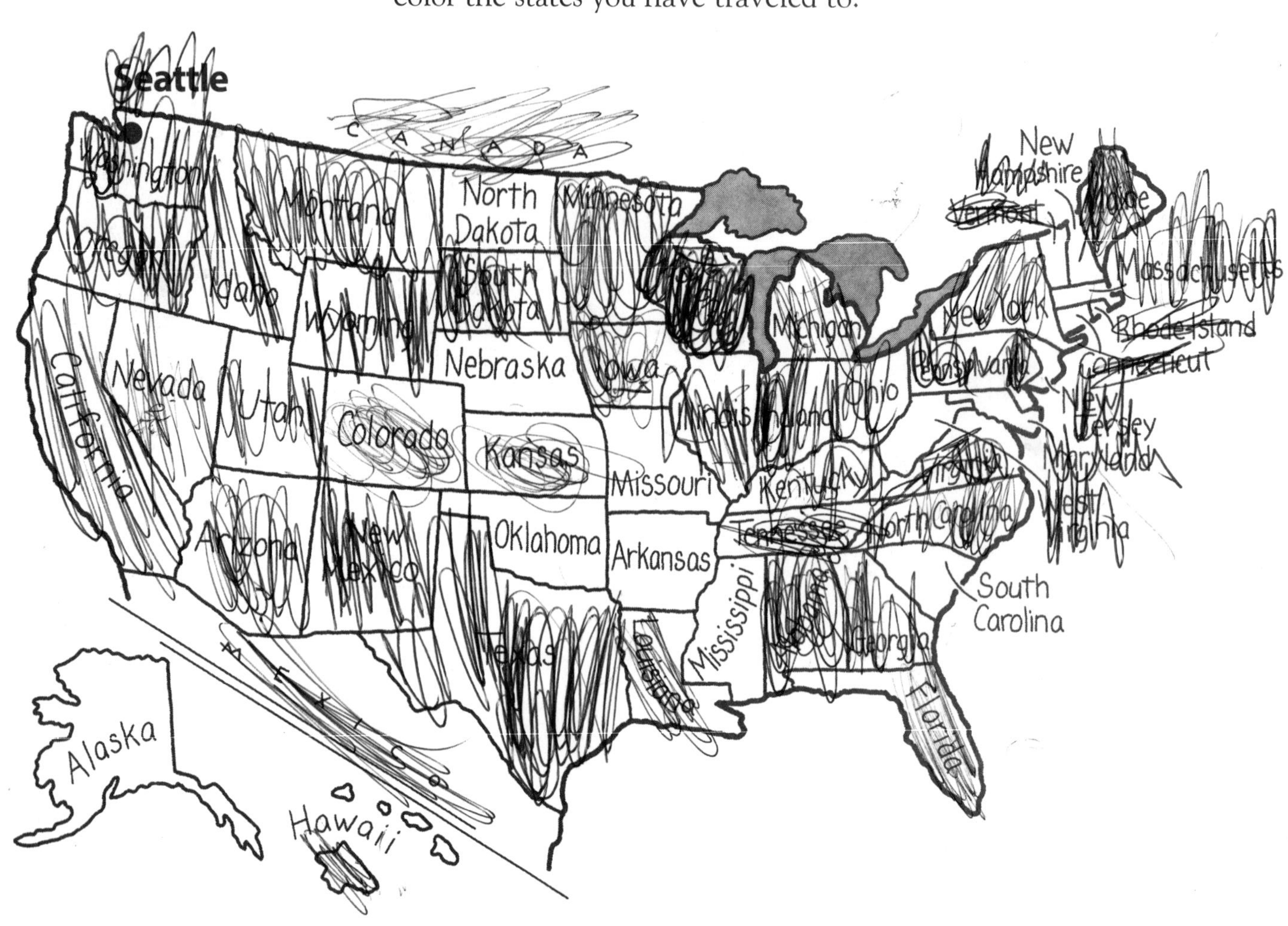

WELCOME TO SEATTLE!

YOU'RE OVERLOOKING A SHIMMERING BAY, dotted with boats. Modern skyscrapers and historic buildings fill the skyline behind you. A breeze from the bay ruffles your hair as a horn blast from a ferry boat drowns out a gull's cry. You and your parents cross the street and catch the Waterfront Streetcar. "Welcome aboard," the motorman says, smiling.

Seattle overlooks beautiful Elliott Bay.

Marc Caryl

Seattle, the largest city in the state of Washington, is in the northwest corner of the United States. On a map, Seattle has an hour-glass shape because it is squeezed between Lake Washington and Elliott Bay—part of Puget Sound. Called the Inland Sea by early explorers, Puget Sound connects to the Pacific Ocean. Seattle's mild, wet climate keeps the landscape green. In fact, Seattle's citizens have nicknamed their home "The Emerald City."

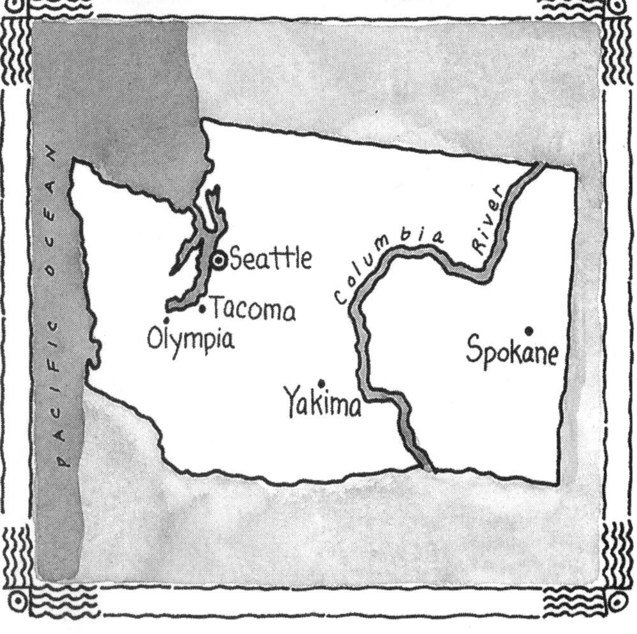

Explorers, Fur Traders, and an Important Chief

Chief Sealth was the leader of the Suquamish and Duwamish Indians who lived around Puget Sound before white people came to America. He was born in 1786 on Blake Island in Puget Sound. As a boy, Sealth watched explorers and fur traders from Russia, Spain, France, England, and finally the American Colonies sail into Puget Sound and march across his tribe's land.

Eventually, settlers began to trickle into the area. Sealth grew up and became chief. He ruled with kindness, but his word was law. He saw that his people's world was changing. In 1854, Chief Sealth spoke with Isaac Stevens, the territorial governor and Indian commissioner. Shortly after that he agreed, with great sadness, to a treaty that turned over Indian land to the U.S. government.

Museum of History & Industry, Seattle

Seattle is named after Chief Sealth.

Duwamish and Suquamish Indians pressed boards to their babies' foreheads to make them flatter. They believed this made people look more attractive.

Seattle's Beginnings

On November 13, 1851, Arthur Denny and his party of 23 settlers sailed into Elliott Bay and settled on Alki Point. They realized they needed a deeper harbor if the settlement was to become an important seaport, so they moved across Elliott Bay to what is now Pioneer Square and part of the downtown area. The settlers named their new town Seattle to honor Chief Sealth, who remained friendly with the settlers until his death in 1866. Seattle is one of the oldest cities on the West Coast.

If you had a chance to rename the city of Seattle, what would you want to call it? Why? Write your new name in the space provided.

THE GREAT FIRE OF 1889

Seattle's fire chief was on vacation, but most of the other 40,000 people who lived and worked in Seattle were in town when a furniture builder left a pot of glue on the stove for too long. First, his glue caught fire, then his shop caught fire. When the fire finally burned itself out about 12 hours later, most of Seattle had burned to the ground.

Pemco Webster & Stevens Collection/Museum of History & Industry, Seattle

The fire started in a furniture maker's shop at 2:30 p.m. . . .

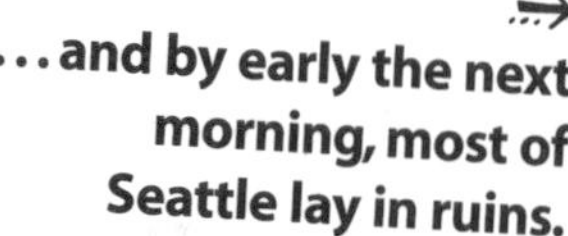

. . . and by early the next morning, most of Seattle lay in ruins.

Museum of History & Industry, Seattle

A Blessing in Disguise

During the ten years before the fire, about 37,000 settlers streamed into Seattle. They all needed places to live right away, so rickety wood buildings were constructed on muddy ground that squished when settlers walked across it. Why was the ground so wet? Pioneer Square was at sea level, which meant there was too much water in the ground to dig holes for building foundations and plumbing.

Unicorn Stock Photos/V. E. Horne

The popular Underground Tour leaves from Pioneer Square.

The Seattle Underground Tour lets you stroll through part of the original city. Another way to see parts of the old city underground is to peer through some of the sidewalk grates in Pioneer Square.

So, after the ashes of the fire had cooled, the citizens started to build new buildings out of brick and stone. To solve the water problem, they raised city streets one story higher, almost like building a second story on your house. In the buildings that survived the fire, first floors became basements and second floors became first floors. It sounds weird, but it worked.

First You See It, Then You Don't

Seattle has lots of hills, but not quite as many as there used to be. In 1898, city planners decided to get rid of Denny Hill. Planners said that a 3,000-foot hill next to the downtown area made it difficult for the city to grow. Engineers considered the problem, and they came up with an unusual solution. Aiming dozens of giant water hoses at the hill, workers slowly turned Denny Hill into a river of mud that rushed down the street and into Elliott Bay. Today, you can get a good look at the city and its hills from Kerry Park or Hamilton Viewpoint.

D. A. Ruehler

Mount Rainier towers above Reflection Lake.

Natural Beauty

Seattle is a city of breathtaking natural beauty. Drivers have been known to bump into the car in front of them because they were looking at the sun setting behind the Olympic Mountains, or rising over the Cascade Mountains, or shining on Mount Rainier. Ski slopes and camping areas are just one hour east of Seattle in the Cascades. Puget Sound and Seattle's three lakes (Lake Washington, Lake Union, and Green Lake) also hold their share of recreation areas. With so much water everywhere, it's no wonder that one out of every six people in Seattle owns a boat—more than in any other state in the U.S.

Mount Rainier was called *Tahoma* by Native Americans. One of their legends tells of how Tahoma used to be part of the Olympic Mountain Range, but the Olympics grew too fast and became too crowded, so Tahoma picked herself up and moved.

Greater Seattle
EDMONDS
Aurora Av
405
5
99
PUGET SOUND
N 105th St
15th AV NW
Hollman RD
N Northgate
513
Green Lake
BALLARD
NE 45th St
Sandpoint WY
NW Market
Salmon Bay Waterway
LAKE WASHINGTON
KIRKLAND
REDMOND
Union Bay
520
MAGNOLIA
QUEEN ANNE
Portage Bay
BELLEVUE
Elliott Av
Lake Union
Alaskan WY
Elliott Bay
Downtown
LAKE SAMMAMISH
Alki Av
Harbor Island
Harbor AV
Mercer Island
90
ALKI
Spokane St
Beach Dr SW
Duwamish Waterway
Boeing Field
ISSAQUAH
99
900
Seattle-Tacoma International Airport
405

Seattle's Most Famous Landmark

Eddie Carlson, the organizer of the 1962 World's Fair in Seattle, first sketched his idea for an attention-getting building for the fairgrounds on a napkin. His unusual idea became Seattle's most famous building, the Space Needle. The Space Needle looks like a flying saucer on three long spindly legs, the total height of which is about 605 feet tall. Its foundation extends four stories underground. Three glass elevators whisk you to a restaurant near the top in an ear-popping 43 seconds, or up another 20 feet to the observation deck. The restaurant level turns slowly, so you can enjoy the view from every direction while seated at your table.

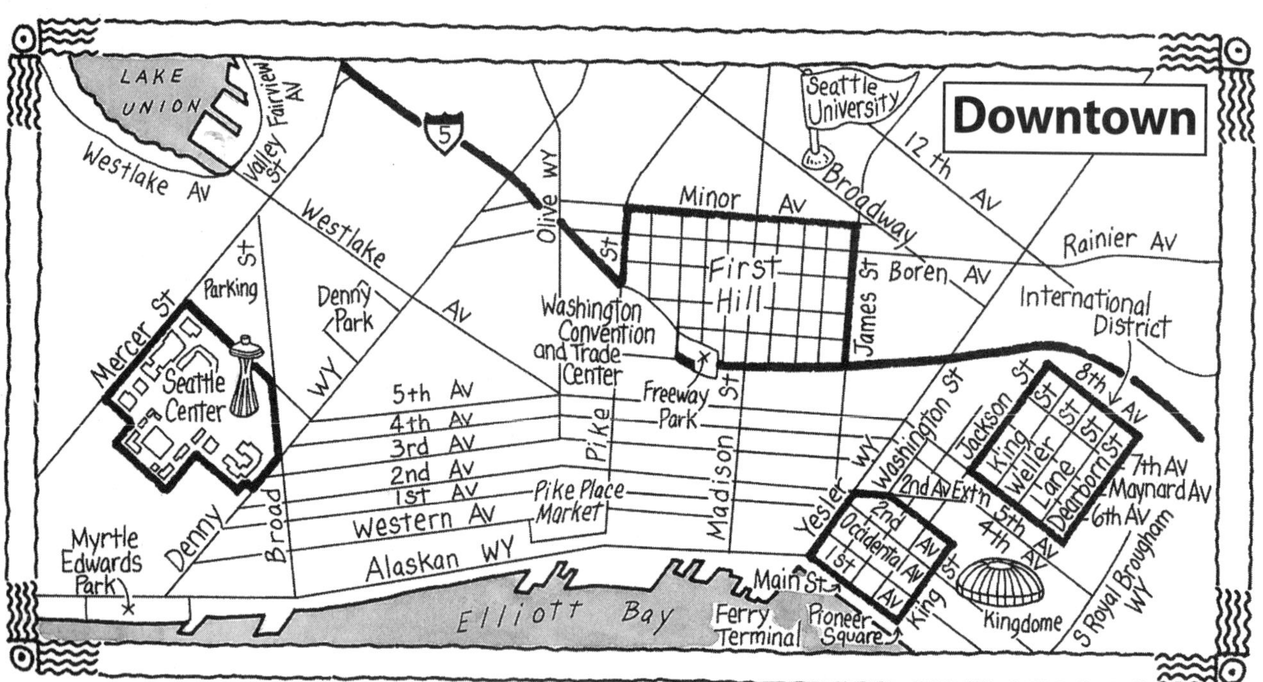

KidStar, an award-winning national radio station, broadcasts from Seattle on 1250 AM. It's a good way to find out what Seattle kids are up to, since many of the announcers are kids.

KidStar Interactive Media Inc.

KidStar announcer Great Scott laughs it up with his guests.

Seattle Artists and Musicians

Living in Seattle must help people become more creative because the city has one of the nation's most active art communities. Musicians such as Jimi Hendrix and Quincy Jones and musical groups such as Pearl Jam and Nirvana began their careers in Seattle. The city also has a symphony and a ballet company. Many writers and artists live and work in Seattle, including the painters Jacob Lawrence and William Cumming. There are also more live theater performances in Seattle each year than in any other city outside New York. One Seattle theater is even devoted to kids.

GOLD IN THE KLONDIKE AND OTHER STRIKE-IT-RICH STORIES

• In 1852, Henry Yesler sailed into town and announced that he planned to build a steam-run saw mill. Cutting and selling timber was Seattle's first big business. Today, electronic equipment, grain, and airplanes have replaced timber as Seattle's most important export. Seattle's port is still one of the top five busiest ports in the U.S.

• In 1897, the steamship *Portland* docked in Seattle carrying almost one ton of gold from the Klondike. The gold rush was on! Even Seattle's mayor quit his job and ran off to Canada to try to get rich. Thousands of people passed through Seattle between 1897 and 1902. Not many prospectors found gold, but Seattle merchants sold $25 million worth of gold-mining equipment in less than a year.

• In 1916, Seattle lumberman Bill Boeing took his first airplane ride and decided he could build a better plane. Today, Boeing is the world's leading airplane manufacturer.

• In 1975, Bill Gates and Paul Allen, two Seattle kids who loved computers, started a computer company called Microsoft. Microsoft now earns more than $8 billion annually.

• In 1993, Bill Nye, a former Boeing engineer, became *Bill Nye the Science Guy* on television. His motto: "Science rules!"

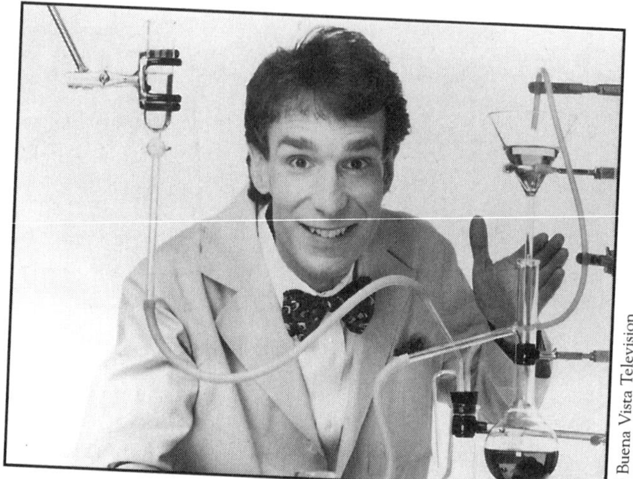

Bill Nye the Science Guy ⇢

GOING FOR THE GOLD

Manny the miner needs your help if he wants to strike it rich. Can you help him find the gold mine?

Seattle Grows Up

Over the past ten years, nearly 5,000 people a year have moved to Seattle. Today, 533,000 people live in the city, enough to fill 12,688 school buses! Seattle-ites watch more movies and read more books than people in other cities of the same size.

But not all people in Seattle are bookworms and theater-goers. Rain or shine, Seattle-ites love to go to festivals like Bumbershoot and SeaFair. And some Seattle-ites like water so much they live on it. There are nearly 500 floating homes on Lake Union and Portage Bay.

Heckler Associates

Getting clammy at Ivar's Fourth of July Party!

Keep Clam!

Seattle has its share of colorful characters. John Doyle Bishop was the shop owner who was sent to jail for painting a green stripe down the street on Saint Patrick's Day. J.P. Patches, the city's beloved clown and television star, used to peek into his "I C You 2" television set to see if his listeners had cleaned their rooms. But Ivar Haglund is the only Seattle citizen (besides Chief Sealth) who had a statue built in his honor. Haglund was a guitar-playing storyteller who owned the Smith Tower and a popular chain of seafood restaurants. He also invented the silly slogan "Keep Clam!" and displayed a windsock in the shape of a carp on the Smith Tower flagpole.

WHERE'S BIG FOOT?

Big Foot, or *Sasquatch*, as the Salish-speaking tribes of the North called him, is said to be a hairy, giant half-man and half-beast. Some folks say Big Foot lives somewhere in Washington. Can you spot him on this page? When you've found him, color the scene.

How Much Does it Rain in Seattle?

The bad news is that it rains a lot. Moisture drizzles, drips, mists or pours from Seattle skies 200 days of the year. But even with all those gray skies, Seattle only gets 38 inches of rainfall per year—less than Atlanta, Boston, New York, or Houston. So don't worry—Seattle-ites don't have webbed feet.

In fact, if you visit Seattle in the warm months of July and August you might even want to bring a little rain with you.

When the sun comes out, Seattle-ites love to use sunglasses. More sunglasses are bought per person in Seattle than in any other city in the U.S.

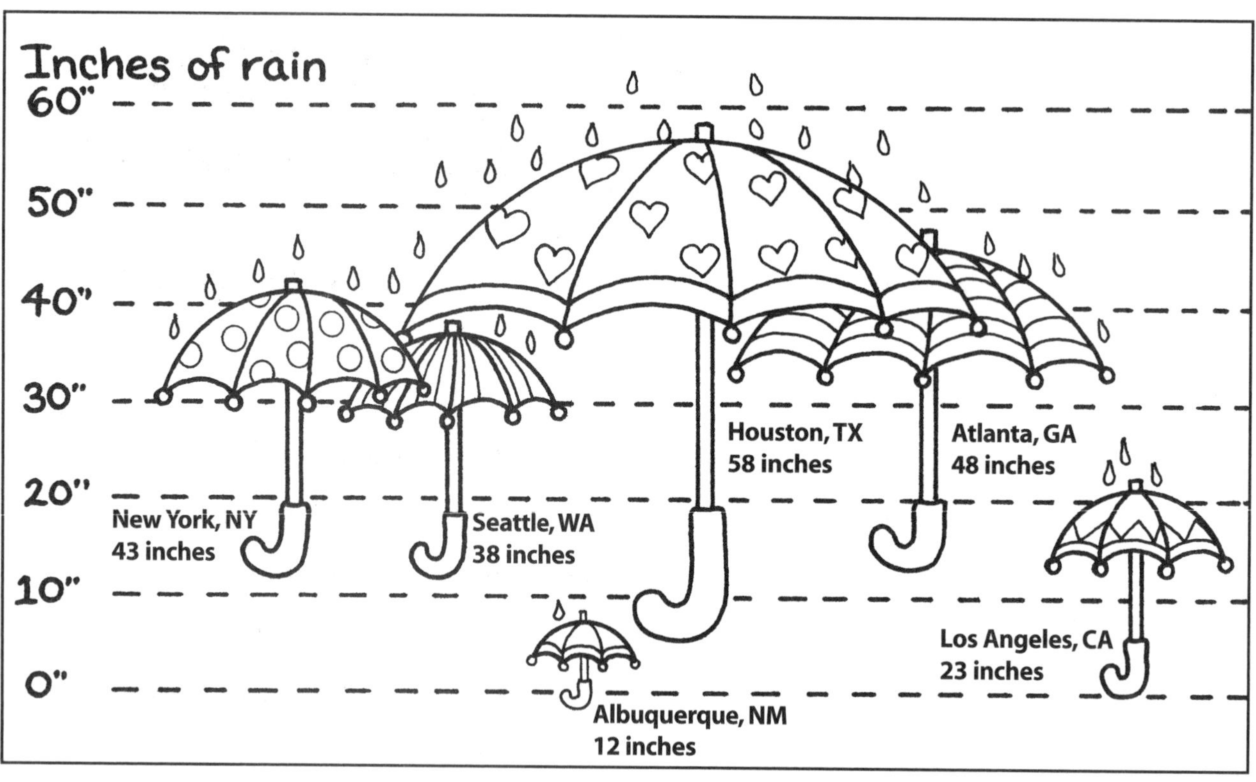

Here are some ideas of what to take when you're out exploring the city!

TRAVEL TIPS

If you visit during the winter, pack warm sweaters and sweatshirts along with long-sleeve shirts and jeans—winter temperatures can often drop to 20 degrees. Seattle's summer temperatures average a pleasant 72 degrees, but don't forget an umbrella and water-repellent jacket for the rain. Bring a backpack for picnics or souvenirs, a map, and the addresses of your friends. You might want to write a postcard as you cruise around Puget Sound on a ferry boat.

2 PARKS AND THE GREAT OUTDOORS

IF YOU LIKE PARKS AND PLAYGROUNDS, you'll have more than 300 to choose from in Seattle. The parks come in all sizes and shapes. Some are tucked into crowded neighborhoods and are so small they are called "pocket parks." Others are so large they are called "urban wildernesses." Many of the parks stretch out along the shores of Puget Sound or Seattle's lakes. Water sports, kite flying, fishing, walking, biking, tennis, and in-line skating are some of the things you can do in the city's parks. So step outside, take a deep breath of evergreen-scented air, and explore the great outdoors.

Seattle-King Co. News Bureau/Nick Gunderson

Bicyclists pedal through Myrtle Edwards Park.

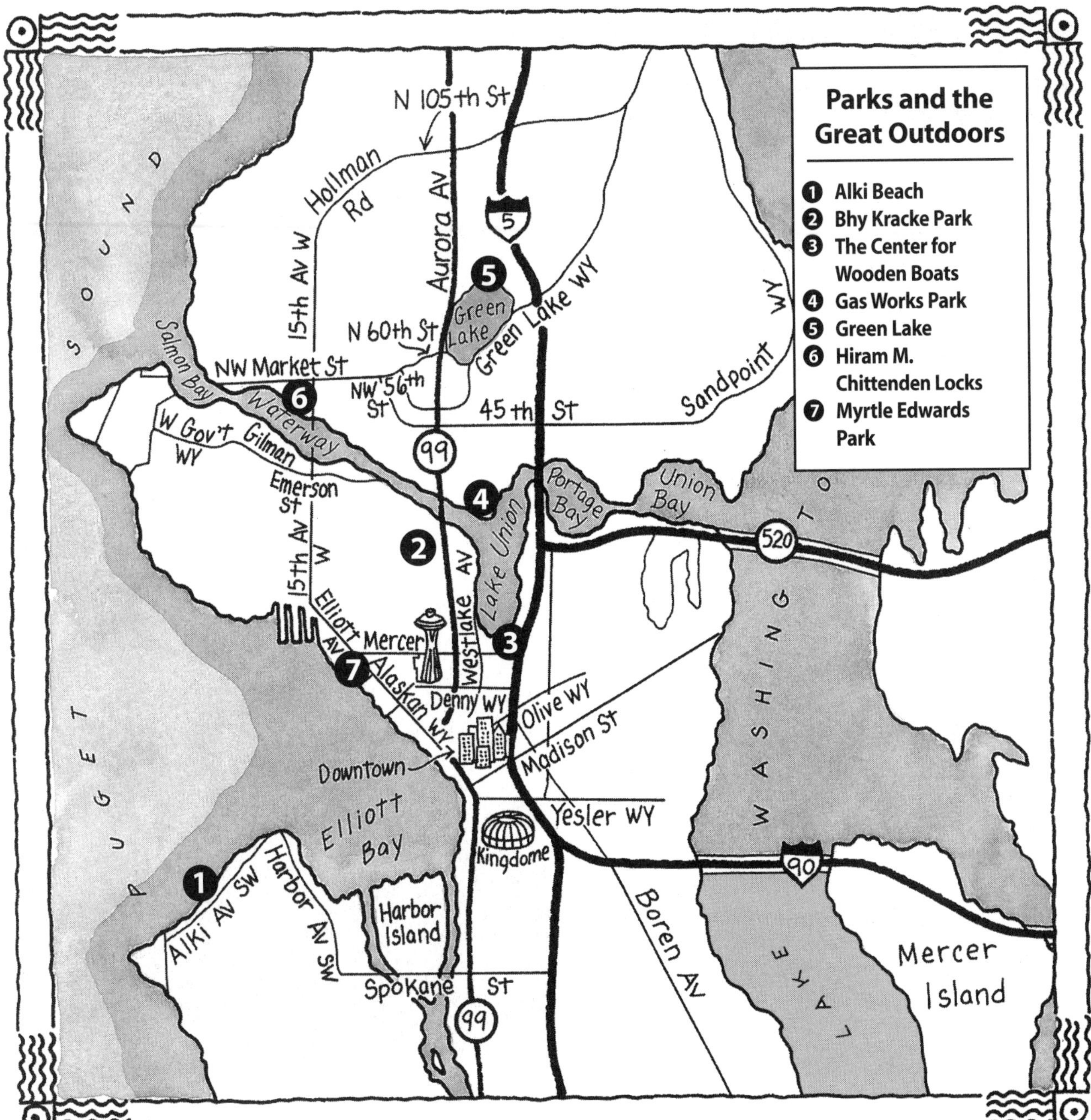
Parks and the Great Outdoors
1 Alki Beach
2 Bhy Kracke Park
3 The Center for Wooden Boats
4 Gas Works Park
5 Green Lake
6 Hiram M. Chittenden Locks
7 Myrtle Edwards Park
N 105th St
Hollman Rd
15th Av W
Aurora Av
5
Green Lake
Green Lake WY
N 60th St
Sandpoint WY
NW Market St
Salmon Bay
Waterway
NW 56th St
45th St
W Gov't WY
Gilman
99
Emerson St
Portage Bay
Union Bay
Lake Union
15th Av W
Westlake Av
520
Elliott Av
Mercer
Alaskan WY
Denny WY
Olive WY
Madison St
Downtown
Yesler WY
Elliott Bay
Kingdome
90
Alki Av SW
Harbor Av SW
Harbor Island
Spokane St
99
Boren Av
Mercer Island
Puget Sound
Lake Washington

BHY KRACKE PARK

A pocket park called Bhy Kracke (by-crack-ee) is a great place to run a little wild in a crowded city. The park is also a great place to take your camera. The views of the Cascade Mountains, Lake Union, and downtown Seattle make excellent photos. Bhy Kracke, one of the city's best-kept secrets, clings to the side of Queen Anne Hill. Even many of the local people don't know it's there because it's sandwiched in between stately old homes. From the upper level of the park, you feel like you can reach out and touch the top of the Space Needle.

Race down the path that winds through the park. Play tag in one of the mini-meadows. Sneak into the sand pit in the lower park. Help your little brother or sister swing through the jungle gym. If you have time, picnic at the park's only picnic table, then climb back up the hill to the parking lot.

Bhy Kracke is a green jewel of a park.

Can you imagine living in a science or algebra classroom? When Queen Anne High School closed, developers turned it into condominiums. Now, from a condo on the fifth floor, you can see all the way to Canada.

The Seattle skyline from Bhy Kracke Park

A PICNIC AT THE PARK

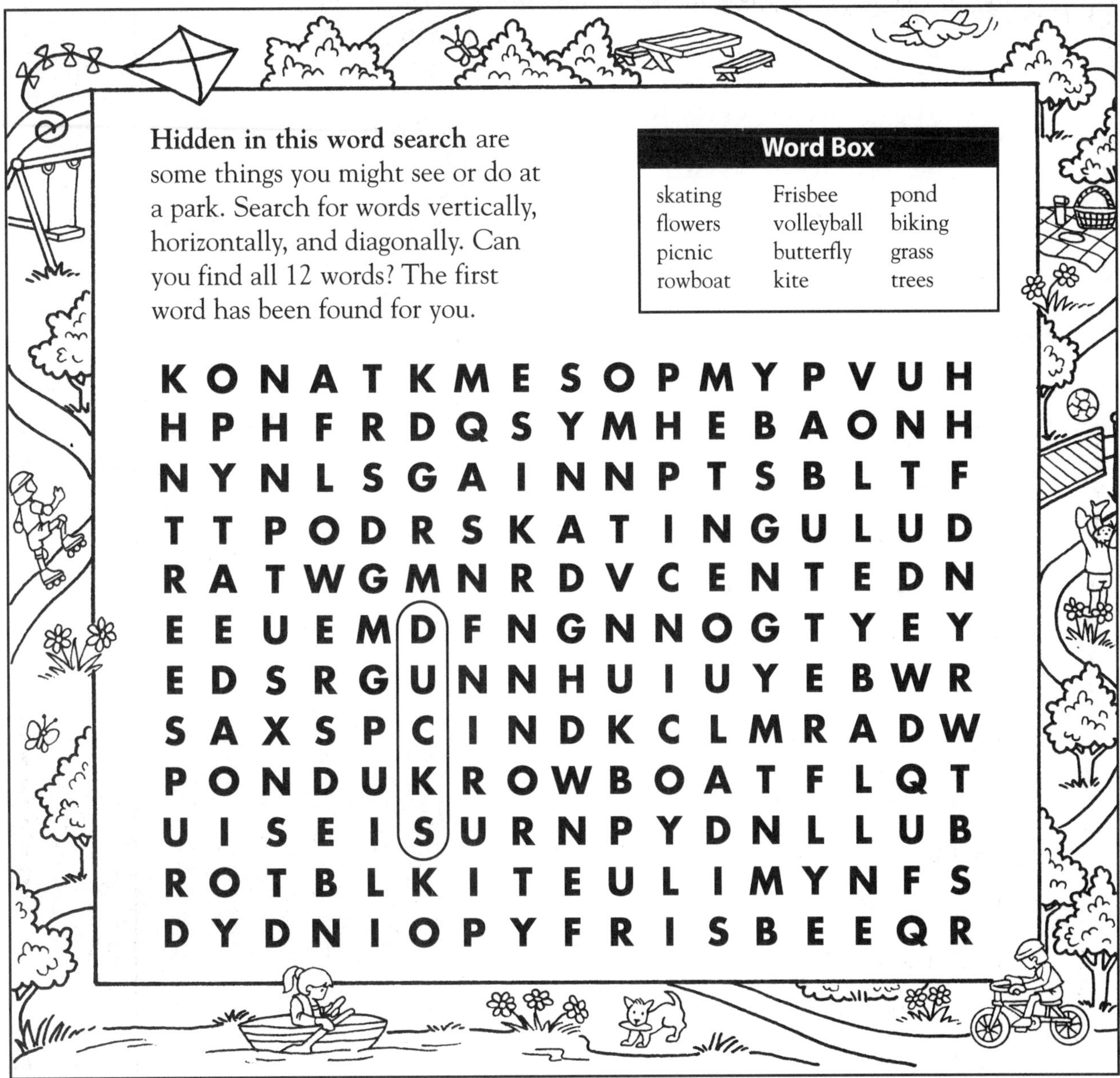

Hidden in this word search are some things you might see or do at a park. Search for words vertically, horizontally, and diagonally. Can you find all 12 words? The first word has been found for you.

Word Box		
skating	Frisbee	pond
flowers	volleyball	biking
picnic	butterfly	grass
rowboat	kite	trees

K O N A T K M E S O P M Y P V U H
H P H F R D Q S Y M H E B A O N H
N Y N L S G A I N N P T S B L T F
T T P O D R S K A T I N G U L U D
R A T W G M N R D V C E N T E D N
E E U E M D F N G N N O G T Y E Y
E D S R G U N N H U I U Y E B W R
S A X S P C I N D K C L M R A D W
P O N D U K R O W B O A T F L Q T
U I S E I S U R N P Y D N L L U B
R O T B L K I T E U L I M Y N F S
D Y D N I O P Y F R I S B E E Q R

U.S. Coast Guard

The Alki Point Light Station

Restaurants sit shoulder to shoulder across the street from the beach. Spud Fish and Chips began in 1935. Back then an order of fish and chips to go cost ten cents.

ALKI BEACH

Alki Beach—where the settlers landed—is just ten minutes from downtown. On the beach volleyball players smack balls, families build beach fires, and sculptors build sand castles. Seagulls scream, sea-lions bark, and scuba divers and kayakers slip into the saltwaters of Puget Sound. Walkers stroll along a path as skaters and bikers race past shouting, "On your right!"

At the west end of the beach stands the **Alki Point Light Station**. The Coast Guard offers tours. A public boat launch, a fishing pier, boat rentals, and impressive views of downtown Seattle mark the east end of the Alki recreational area. If you're lucky, you might see a pod of orcas. They often swim down from the San Juan Islands to see what there is to eat.

CONNECT THE DOTS

From Alki Beach in Seattle, you can sometimes see Orca whales swimming past. Connect the dots to catch a glimpse of an orca, then color in the scene.

MYRTLE EDWARDS PARK

A perfect place for in-line skating, Myrtle Edwards Park follows the shores of Elliott Bay. The paths, one for bikers and one for walkers, are safe and wide. You can start out at Pier 70 on the waterfront and head north. You might want to tuck a fishing pole under your arm. Pier 86, about a mile down the park, is a fishing pier complete with a bait and tackle shop. Kids under 14 can fish without a license in Washington State any time, on any public dock.

Benches and a view of the water make this park another good picnic spot. On the Fourth of July it's the place to be for front-row seats to the Ivar Haglund fireworks display over Elliott Bay.

Space Needle Corporation

The Space Needle turns into a "sparkler" for the New Year's Eve fireworks show.

The gigantic silos next to the park are part of a grain terminal. Spouts shoot grain into waiting ships, but no grain dust clouds the air. Anti-pollution controls make this the cleanest grain terminal in the U.S.

WHAT'S THE DIFFERENCE?

These two pictures might look the same, but they are not. How many differences between the two scenes can you find? Hint: There are at least 15 differences.

HIRAM M. CHITTENDEN LOCKS

This **Ballard District** park is a grassy picnic area surrounding the Hiram Chittenden Locks. The locks make this park unusual. Early settlers dreamed of floating harvested logs across Lake Washington and Lake Union to Puget Sound. In 1906, workers began digging an eight-mile ship canal between the lakes and the sound to make the dream a reality. Because the lakes are 26 feet higher than Puget Sound, locks were needed for a ship to make the journey. Locks work like water elevators. A boat enters a lock and an engineer either adds water to the lock to raise the ship up to the canal, or drains water from the lock to lower the ship down to the sound. Visitors line the walkways at the locks to watch more than 100,000 commercial or pleasure boats pass through the locks each year.

A fish ladder next to the locks allows salmon to return to their spawning grounds. The ladder is glass-sided so you can watch fish climb each step of the way. Grass and picnic areas surround the locks.

Seattle-King Co. News Bureau/Nick Gunderson

Boats at the Chittenden Locks

MIXED-UP PICTURE STORY

This picture story should show a boat going through the Hiram M. Chittenden Locks. Unfortunately, the pictures are out of order. Put the scene in the correct order by filling in the number box in the bottom left-hand corner of each picture.

GREEN LAKE

Green Lake is a small lake, but it's a big center for outdoor activity. You can walk, jog, skate, and bike around the paved three-mile path that rims the lake. Or you can rent a boat to paddle or row across the lake, or go fishing. **Gregg's Green Lake Cycle** rents bikes and the Seattle Parks department rents boats. If you're into water sports, swim in an indoor pool. At the south end of the lake, there's a **Pitch and Putt** miniature golf course and tennis courts. On the west side, you can try out lawn bowling. The tiny island in the middle of the lake is reserved for ducks only.

Wide rolling lawns around the lake make good picnic spots. But if picnics aren't your thing, **Guido's Pizza** or **Spud Fish and Chips** across the street serve tasty food.

Seattle Department of Parks and Recreation sets aside one Saturday and one Sunday each month as Bicycle Day. Certain areas of the city are blocked off for bikers—no motor vehicles allowed.

Seattle-King Co. News Bureau/Nick Gunderson

Boating and fishing are popular activities at Green Lake.

CROSSWORD FUN

There are lots of ways to have fun at the park. Solve this crossword by figuring out the clues or completing the sentences. If you need help, use the clue box.

Across

1. Cinderella went to one of these, but you can also hit it with a racquet.
2. If you want to catch a fish at Green Lake, you need a fishing _____.
3. Bring food and a blanket to the park if you want to have one of these.
5. The Gas Works Park has lots of wind, which is perfect for flying a _____.
7. Unless it has a flat tire, riding one of these two-wheelers is fun.
8. If you're in a hurry, you can run. If not, then you can _____.

Down

1. Sit down on a park _____ if you feel tired.
3. It might have a weird name, but Seattle's Bhy Kracke _____ is worth a visit.
4. You can take photos of your family if you bring one of these.
6. These leafy giants provide shade for people and animals.

Clue Box

bike	trees
park	bench
ball	pole
kite	picnic
walk	camera

GAS WORKS PARK

Gas Works Park on the north shore of Lake Union is the weirdest park you're likely to see, so take your camera. The park used to be a gas plant. The once-rusting maze of pipes, boilers, and engines now sports coats of paint in a rainbow of colors and is a jungle-gym that would challenge Tarzan. A sky-lighted roof covers the area, which is like a huge barn. Grassy fields and picnic grounds surround the play barn. A man-made hill, perfect for flying kites, is nearby. Even if you don't fly a kite, climb the hill to see the do-it-yourself sundial.

The **Burke-Gilman Trail** for bikers and walkers starts at Gas Works Park.

Follow the directions for the sundial at the top of Gas Works' grassy hill. Your body will cast a shadow toward the hour markers on the edge of the dial. Can you tell what time it is?

Paul Otteson

The colorful and odd Gas Works Park

UNTANGLE THE KITES

**Can you figure out which kite belongs to each kite flyer?
Match the kite with the person flying it by tracing the kite strings.**

THE CENTER FOR WOODEN BOATS

Do you want to be captain of your own ship? The Center for Wooden Boats at the south end of Lake Union has rowboats, canoes, and sailboats for rent. You'll be asked to demonstrate your boating skills before renting one. As you and your family paddle or sail around the lake, watch for the floating homes moored next to the shore, and listen for the roar of seaplanes taking off and landing.

After your boat ride, stop by the Center's museum to find out everything you ever wanted to know about wooden boats. Or spend time at the Center's boat shop to watch the staff restore or build traditional boats. On Fourth of July weekend, the center has a **Wooden Boats Festival** with activities especially for kids, including boat building, sail mending, and other maritime skills.

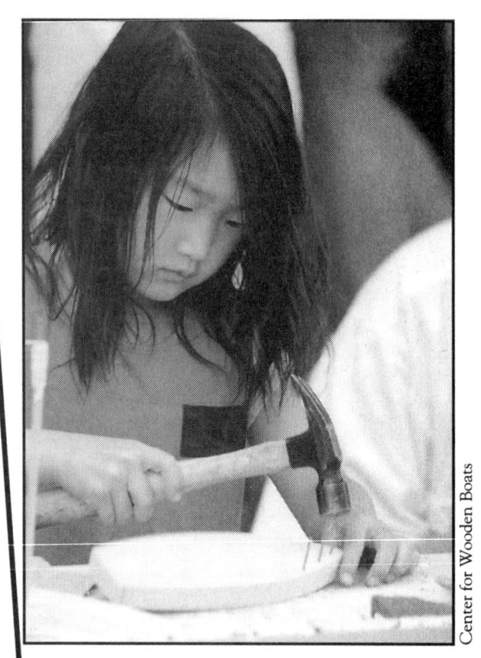

Center for Wooden Boats

A visitor practices her boat-building skills.

Center for Wooden Boats

The Center is located on Lake Union.

MY TRAVEL JOURNAL

—Parks and the Great Outdoors—

I had fun when I visited: ______________________________

I learned about: ______________________________

My favorite park was: ______________________________

What I enjoyed doing the most was: ______________________________

This is a picture of what I saw at a park in Seattle

3 ANIMALS AROUND SEATTLE

"WHAT IS MAN WITHOUT THE BEASTS?" Chief Sealth said long ago. "If all the beasts were gone, man would die from a great loneliness of spirit. For whatever happens to the beasts, soon happens to man. All things are connected."

The people of Seattle believed Chief Sealth's words and made sure that many different kinds of animals will always have a home in the area. Today, owls are still heard calling from the tops of Seattle's fir trees. Herons fly from their nesting grounds along the Duwamish River to fish at Alki Beach. Hippopotamuses splash in their pool at the zoo. If you are someone who enjoys animals, you'll have an easy time finding them in Seattle.

Woodland Park Zoo/Richard Wilhelm

A Kodiak bear at the Woodland Park Zoo

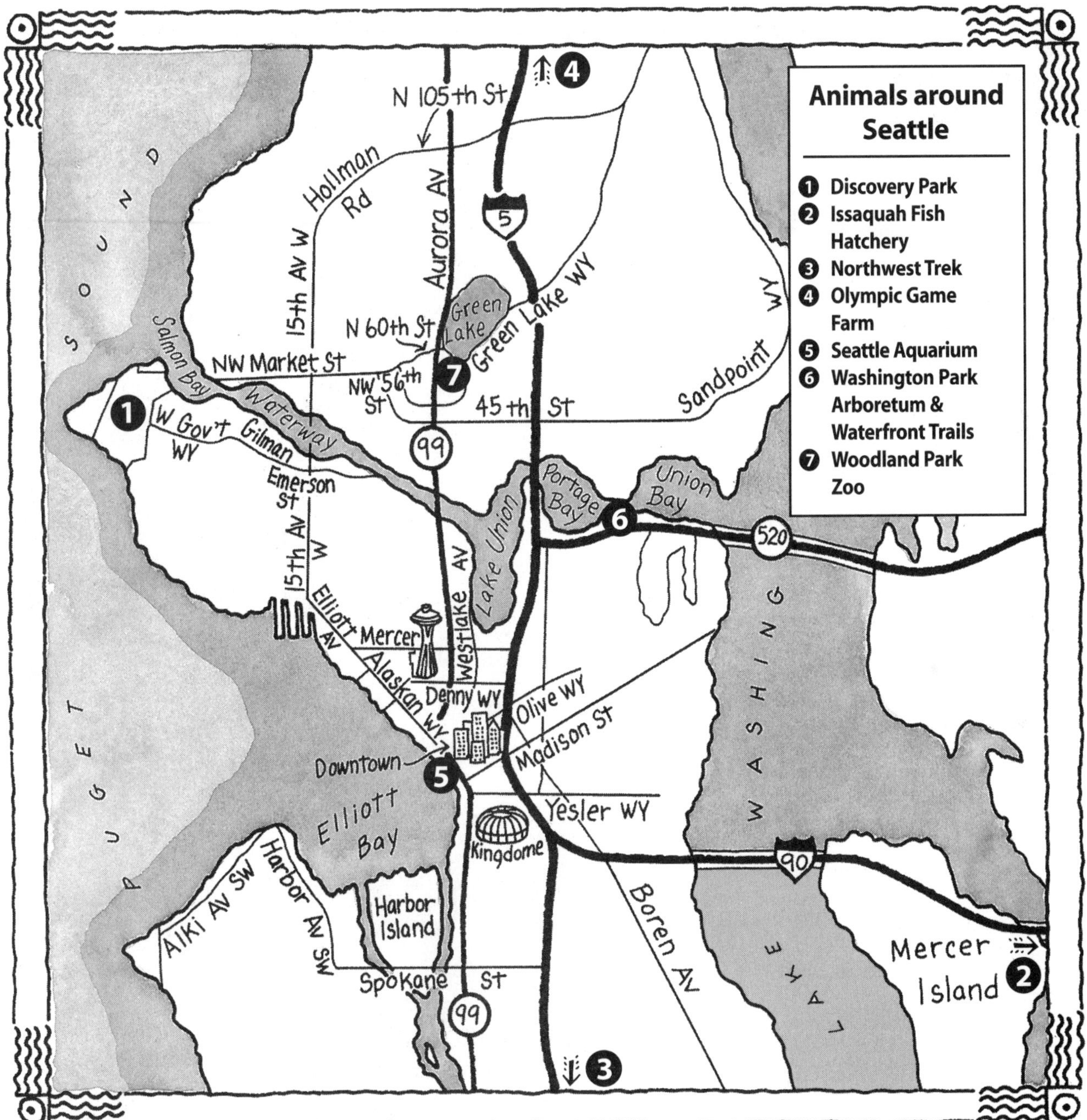
Animals around Seattle
1 Discovery Park
2 Issaquah Fish Hatchery
3 Northwest Trek
4 Olympic Game Farm
5 Seattle Aquarium
6 Washington Park Arboretum & Waterfront Trails
7 Woodland Park Zoo
PUGET SOUND
N 105th St
Hollman Rd
15th Av W
Aurora Av
5
Green Lake
Green Lake WY
N 60th St
NW Market St
Salmon Bay
Waterway
NW 56th St
45th St
Sandpoint WY
W Gov't WY
Gilman
99
Emerson St
Portage Bay
Union Bay
Lake Union
520
15th Av W
Elliott Av
Mercer
Westlake Av
Alaskan WY
Denny WY
Olive WY
Madison St
Downtown
Elliott Bay
Kingdome
Yesler WY
LAKE WASHINGTON
90
Boren Av
Alki Av SW
Harbor Av SW
Harbor Island
Spokane St
99
Mercer Island

SEATTLE AQUARIUM

Seattle Aquarium is like a window onto Puget Sound. Award-winning exhibits of Pacific Northwest sea life make you feel part of the action. Step into the **Underwater Dome.** In an enormous 400,000 gallon tank, sea creatures swim above you and all around. Watch as a spiny dogfish snatches up a fish for dinner. You'll feel as if you are walking on the ocean floor. Divers feed the animals in the dome every day around 1:30 p.m.

Seals, sea lions, and otters play in open air tanks. If you're lucky, you might see a trainer brushing a seal's teeth. Sandpipers and other sea birds hop about in naturalistic settings. You can watch salmon climb the aquarium's fish ladder as they return from the ocean. Fluffy, the aquarium's six-foot-long water monitor lizard, stares at you from its pond. At the **Touch Tank**, starfish and featherduster worms tickle the palm of your hand when you pick them up.

Starfish and other squishy creatures live in the Touch Tank.

Seattle Aquarium/Leo J. Shaw

A diver peers out of the Underwater Dome as visitors look in.

Seattle Aquarium/Leo J. Shaw

The world's largest species of octopus, the mottled red cephalopod lurks 100 feet off shore at Golden Gardens Park.

Otters sunning themselves at Golden Gardens Park

Seattle Aquarium/C.J. Casson

Without telling anyone what you're doing, ask for a word to fill in each blank. For example, "Give me an action word." When all the blanks are filled in, read the story out loud. One blank has been filled in for you.

The Octopus Who Changed the Oceans

Once, _______ (number) years ago, the world's oceans were _______ (color). Then, an octopus named _______ (name) was born. This octopus was _______ (describing word), with spots, and _______ (describing word) arms that stretched in every direction. The octopus was very angry (emotion), because he didn't _______ (action word) visitors. One day a _______ (animal) was swimming near the octopus' favorite _______ (place 1). This new visitor made the octopus very _______ (emotion) because the swimmer was stealing all the octopus' _______ (things). So, the octopus took a deep breath and _______ (action word)ed until the entire Pacific became _______ (color). So, remember—never _______ (action word) with an octopus' _______ (place 1)!

WASHINGTON PARK ARBORETUM & WATERFRONT TRAILS

The Arboretum offers 250 acres of wetlands to explore. The big question is whether you want to walk, row, or paddle. If you choose to walk, a good place to start is on one of the trails that begin at the Museum of History and Industry. **The Union Bay Waterfront Trail** takes you under the Montlake Bridge and to the Seattle Yacht Club. **The Foster Island Trail**, with its series of wooden bridges, takes you to Marsh and Foster Islands. If you choose to explore by water, the **University of Washington Waterfront Activity Center** will rent your family a boat.

Whether you glide along on the water in a canoe or follow a trail, you'll see plenty of nesting Canadian geese, blue herons, frogs on lily pads, and maybe even a turtle sunning itself.

If you'd like to learn more about Pacific Northwest wetlands and marshes, read *Squish! A Wetland Walk* by Nancy Luenn.

Paul Otteson

Foster Island Trail at the Arboretum

Paul Otteson

Turtles and other wetlands animals thrive at the Arboretum.

CONNECT THE DOTS

Lots of people who visit the Washington Park Arboretum use boats when they want to explore. Connect the dots, then color in the scene.

WOODLAND PARK ZOO

You won't find many animals in cages at this zoo. In fact, sometimes you have to look twice if you want to spot the animals at all! Woodland Park Zoo lets animals live in their own habitats. Going to this zoo is like going on an African safari. Giraffes, lions, and zebras wander around the Savannah. In Tropical Asia, elephants take baths or roll logs, just as they might do in the wild. In the Tropical Rain Forest, poison dart frogs, sloths, and gorillas enjoy life in natural settings. Peacocks roam the zoo grounds, welcoming visitors with their ear-piercing cries.

There are other areas to visit and a petting zoo, too. As the zoo's motto puts it, "We get wilder every year!"

Woodland Park Zoo/Agnes Overbaugh

This Siamang ape swings through the Trail of Vines exhibit.

The Tropical Rain Forest exhibit is home to this ocelot.

Woodland Park Zoo/Milt Huffman

LOOKING AROUND THE ZOO

Hidden in this word search are some things you might see at the Woodland Park Zoo. Search for words vertically, horizontally, and diagonally. Can you find all 11 words? The first one has been found for you.

S	C	F	I	R	Z	S	F	R	O	G	R	L	F
W	L	N	A	L	K	M	E	S	O	P	A	Y	N
E	O	O	R	A	N	G	U	T	A	N	E	A	M
L	O	N	T	S	S	I	A	M	O	N	L	P	B
E	B	P	O	H	E	L	S	L	B	S	O	E	L
P	E	T	A	G	L	K	E	R	I	E	Y	A	E
H	A	L	R	I	L	A	M	G	N	Z	O	C	T
A	C	S	R	G	I	R	A	F	F	E	T	O	L
N	H	O	I	S	H	S	U	Q	U	B	M	C	I
T	G	A	L	L	I	G	A	T	O	R	R	K	O
S	A	V	A	N	N	A	H	N	P	A	D	N	N

Word Box

giraffe
lion
alligator
frog
sloth
zebra
peacock
orangutan
savannah
safari
elephant

A zookeeper invented the "raisin log" to keep his orangutans from getting bored. The raisin log is a piece of wood with holes drilled in it and raisins stuffed into the holes. The orangutans spend hours happily picking out the raisins. ⇛

DISCOVERY PARK

"Yap, yap, yoweeee!" sing the coyotes who live in Seattle. Seattle is also home to red foxes, opossums, raccoons, bald eagles, and many other species of wildlife. Some of these wild creatures live in a wilderness area called Discovery Park about five minutes from downtown. On Saturday, park naturalists will lead you on free nature walks. Discover how snakes slither. Learn how spider webs are stronger than steel and which bats live in Washington. Explore the park's ponds for water bugs, and keep an eye out for owls and eagles taking flight.

The 500-acre park is a former U.S. Army base. It includes forest, meadowland, Puget Sound beach, playing fields, and picnic areas. There are also several nature trails worth investigating.

Barr Lake State Park, CO

Red foxes like this one live at Discovery Park.

Daybreak Star Cultural Center at Discovery Park displays sculptures and murals of mythical animals and birds. One cedar panel tells the legend of Wi-Gyt, a supernatural creature with black wings and magical powers.

WI-GYT RETURNS

Wi-Gyt is a magical, supernatural creature in American Indian folklore. Draw Wi-Gyt according to how you think he might look. What sorts of magical powers do you think he has?

Two floating bridges cross Lake Washington. Evergreen Point Bridge is the longest floating bridge in the world—nearly a mile and a half long!

Issaquah Fish Hatchery

Salmon climb a fish ladder at the hatchery.

ISSAQUAH FISH HATCHERY

Salmon have to accomplish a lot in their short lives. They can live up to four years, but most young salmon don't survive to old age. Predators try to eat them. Dams confuse them. Salmon have to swim 1,000 miles, from the freshwater streams where they were born to Puget Sound and finally the Pacific Ocean. Four years later, if they haven't become a fisherman's prize or a larger fish's meal, salmon find their way home to spawn and die.

Take the I-90 floating bridge to Issaquah, home to one of Washington State's 87 fish hatcheries. Issaquah is about 11 miles east of Seattle. Depending on the time of year you visit, you'll see fish in various stages of their life cycle—from hatching eggs to their return at the end of their lives. There are outdoor ponds, an indoor aquarium, and lots of signs at the Hatchery that explain what's going on.

SAVE THE SALMON!

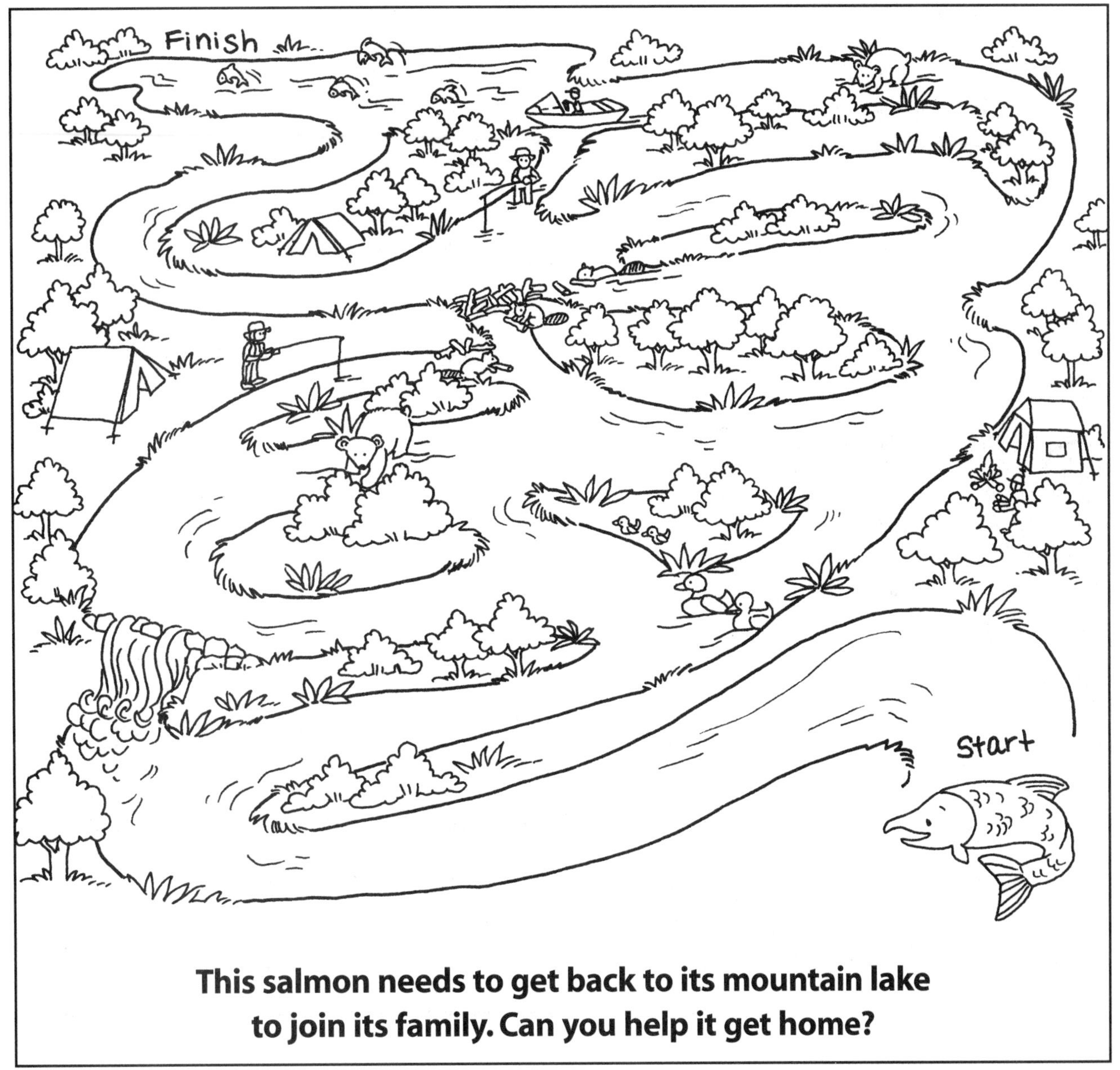

This salmon needs to get back to its mountain lake to join its family. Can you help it get home?

NORTHWEST TREK

Even though it's a long drive from Seattle, you might want to visit Northwest Trek. Located 55 miles south of the city, Northwest Trek lets you experience wildlife up close in forest and meadow settings. From a park tram driven by entertaining naturalist guides, you'll see American bison, caribou, bighorn sheep, elk, black-tailed deer, and mountain goats roaming free. You might even see baby animals taking their first steps.

A walking tour of the park brings you face to face with black bears, grizzly bears, wolves, cougars, raccoons, and birds of prey such as eagles and owls. In the **Cheney Discovery Center**, you get to pet frogs, hold a snake, and watch thousands of bees in a working beehive. After exploring the wilderness, you and your family might want to stop by the Northwest Trek's **Fir Bough Cafe** (the burgers are excellent) or sit at an outdoor picnic table with your lunch.

Northwest Trek

A see-through beehive at Northwest Trek

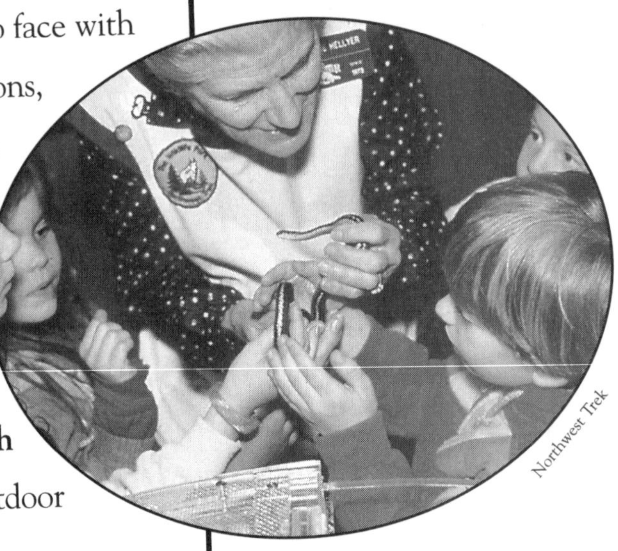

Northwest Trek

Kids meet wildlife up close at Northwest Trek.

CROSSWORD FUN

You can find lots of animals at Northwest Trek. Solve this crossword by figuring out the clues or completing the sentences. If you need help, use the clue box.

Clue Box

elk	wolf
caribou	cougar
grizzly	snakes
bison	eagles

Across

2. This fast, furry animal is also called a mountain lion.
3. The giant ________ bear is more interested in salmon than in you.
6. There are many of these reptiles in Washington, but they aren't poisonous.
7. This animal is the ancient ancestor of most dogs.

Down

1. Not only are these birds our national mascot, they also live at Northwest Trek.
2. This animal is also known as a reindeer. It lives mostly in cold regions.
4. This deer-relative is sometimes hunted for its antlers.
5. Some people call them buffalo, but their real name is _______.

OLYMPIC GAME FARM

The Olympic Game Farm in Sequim on the Olympic Peninsula is home to furry film stars. For 40 years, many animals from the farm have starred on television and in movies such as *Never Cry Wolf*, *The Incredible Journey*, and *The Life and Times of Grizzly Adams*. Hand-raised from birth, the animals are trained to perform with actors and have to be comfortable around people and cameras. The farm works with Walt Disney Studios.

You'll see more than 40 different animals on the guided tour of the farm, including zebra, lions, bear, elk, wolves, llamas, and ostrich. You'll also see movie sets, man-made dens, an aquarium, and a studio barn. You can feed some of the animals at the petting zoo.

Olympic Game Farm owner Lloyd Beebe with Sam, star of Ford/Mercury car commercials.

Olympic Game Farm

Bozo played Ben in *The Life and Times of Grizzly Adams.*

Olympic Game Farm

MY TRAVEL JOURNAL

—Animals around Seattle—

I had fun when I visited: ______________________________

I learned about: ______________________________

____

My favorite animal was: ______________________________

What I enjoyed doing the most was: ______________________________

This is a picture of an animal I saw

4 LANDMARKS, SKYSCRAPERS, AND THE ARTS

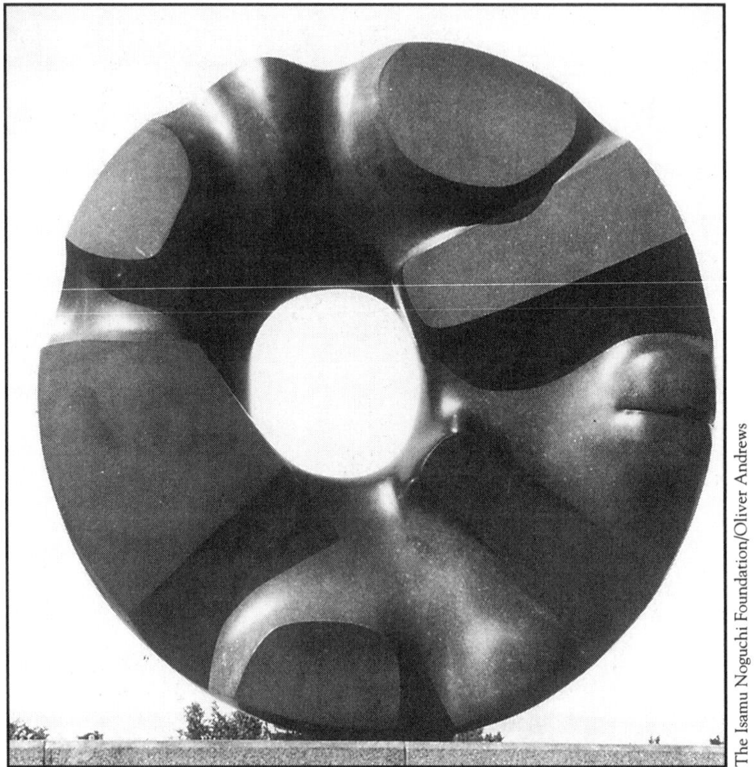

The Isamu Noguchi Foundation/Oliver Andrews

Black Sun, **by artist Isamu Noguchi, is nine feet in diameter.**

SEE A SCULPTURE CALLED *Black Sun* that looks like a giant black doughnut or feel the spray from a roaring waterfall that's really a fountain (you can even walk through it!). Thanks to Seattle's "One Percent for Art" program (one percent of the cost of a new city building goes toward art), Seattle has more public art than any other U.S. city of its size. Even some of the manhole covers in the streets are decorated by artists.

Many of Seattle's buildings are also works of art. Architects from around the world have created unique buildings from brick, concrete, stone, steel, and glass. At night, the lighted windows light up the Seattle sky like stars.

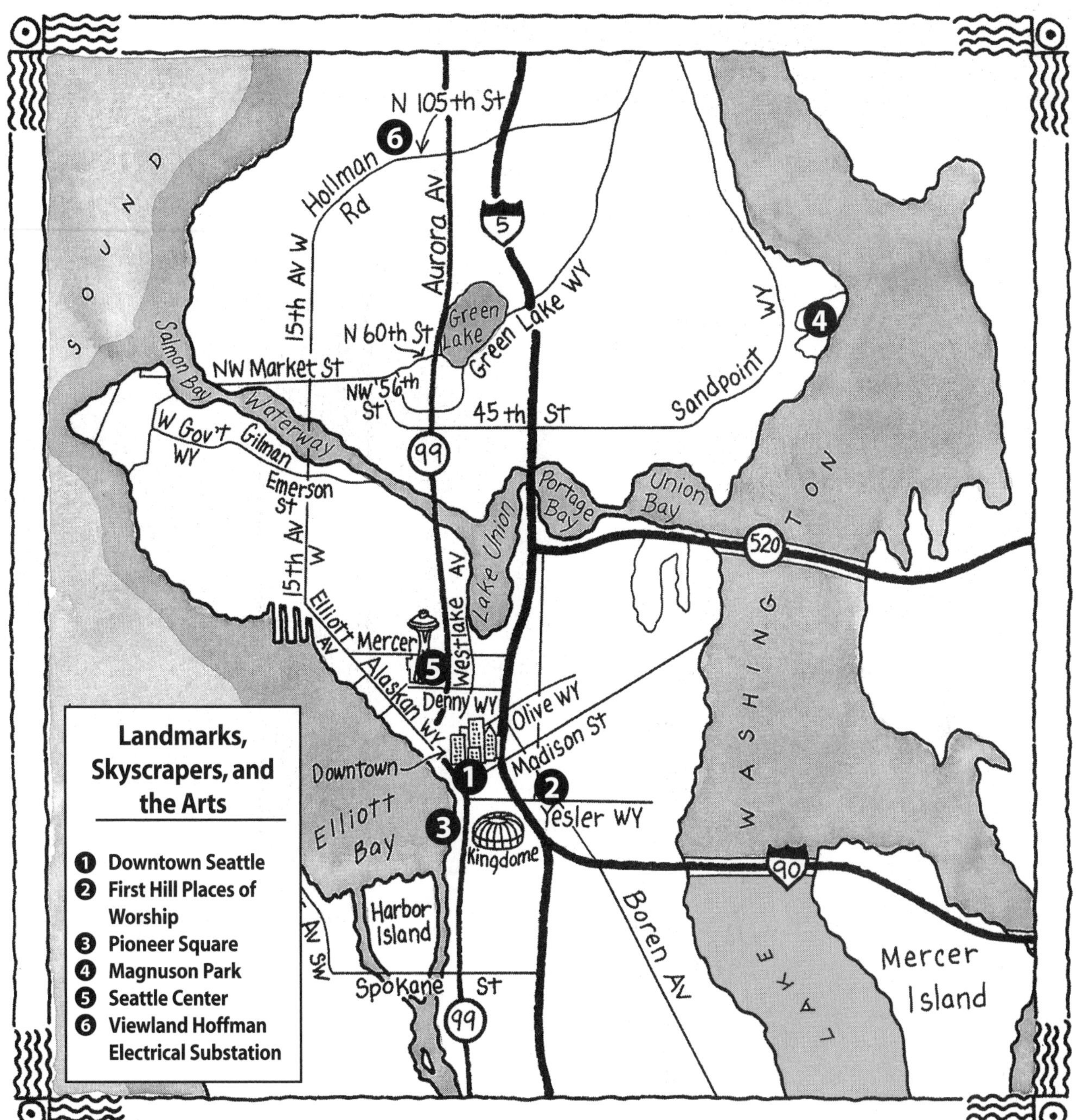

Landmarks, Skyscrapers, and the Arts
1 Downtown Seattle
2 First Hill Places of Worship
3 Pioneer Square
4 Magnuson Park
5 Seattle Center
6 Viewland Hoffman Electrical Substation
SOUND
N 105th St
Hollman Rd
Aurora AV
15th AV W
5
Green Lake
Green Lake WY
N 60th St
NW Market St
NW 56th St
45th St
Sandpoint WY
Salmon Bay
Waterway
W Gov't Gilman WY
Emerson St
99
Portage Bay
Union Bay
520
Lake Union
Westlake AV
15th AV W
Elliott AV
Mercer
Alaskan WY
Denny WY
Olive WY
Madison St
Downtown
Yesler WY
Elliott Bay
Kingdome
90
Harbor Island
Boren AV
Spokane St
99
LAKE WASHINGTON
Mercer Island

PIONEER SQUARE

If you're ready to step into another world, head for United Parcel's **Waterfall Park** in Pioneer Square. It's a magical place with a tumbling waterfall and trickling stream. The park itself is a work of art!

There's more art in **Occidental Park** where four carved totem poles stare out at you. Up the street at **Glass House Art**, glass blowers, working in front of furnaces heated to 2,000 degrees, create glass in a rainbow of colors.

Seattle's first skyscraper, Pioneer Square's **Smith Tower**, looks small when compared with today's buildings. But when the 42-story tower opened in 1914, it was the tallest building in the United States outside of New York City. For a great view, ride the Tower's "gilded-cage" elevator to the observation deck on the 35th floor. From there you can gaze up at the **Columbia Seafirst Center**. The Center is Seattle's tallest building—76 floors of steel and black glass.

Glasshouse Studio

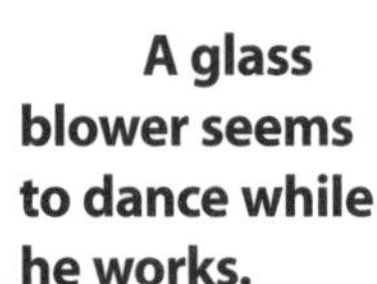

A glass blower seems to dance while he works.

UPS

Waterfall Park

GOING DOWNTOWN

Hidden in this word search are some things you might see on a trip to Pioneer Square in Downtown Seattle. Search for words vertically, horizontally, and diagonally. Can you find all 10 words? The first word has been found for you.

T	O	N	A	T	K	F	U	R	N	A	C	E	L	V
O	P	H	G	R	D	Q	S	Y	M	H	E	L	A	O
W	O	N	A	L	K	M	E	S	O	P	A	Y	P	G
E	B	H	F	R	A	Q	S	Y	M	F	E	B	A	O
R	U	N	L	S	G	S	I	N	R	P	T	S	B	L
P	S	P	O	D	R	S	S	E	B	T	O	T	E	M
O	A	T	T	G	M	N	T	D	V	C	E	N	T	E
U	E	U	A	M	D	A	M	G	N	N	O	G	T	Y
S	D	S	X	G	W	N	N	H	U	I	U	Y	E	C
Q	A	F	I	P	C	I	N	D	K	C	L	M	R	L
O	M	Y	J	U	E	L	E	V	A	T	O	R	F	O
U	I	S	E	I	S	U	R	N	P	Y	D	N	L	C
R	O	S	I	D	E	W	A	L	K	L	I	M	Y	K
S	K	Y	S	C	R	A	P	E	R	I	G	B	E	T

Word Box

waterfall
tower
glass
furnace
totem
elevator
skyscraper
clock
bus
sidewalk

DOWNTOWN SEATTLE

You might enjoy a short art tour of downtown Seattle. A bronze sculpture that looks like three gigantic dinosaur bones sits in front of the Fourth Avenue Building. The sculpture, called ***Vertebrae***, is nicknamed "Bones." English sculptor Henry Moore designed it.

To see a jungle in the city, or if you want to climb up a roaring waterfall, visit **Freeway Park**. The park, with its vines, trees, bushes, and grass, was built over a section of the I-5 freeway. Across from the park you'll see **Naramore Fountain**, created by Seattle's George Tsutakawa.

Although it's not downtown, Seattle-ites love the sculpture called ***Waiting for the Interurban***. They even decorate it whenever they get the chance.

Some of Seattle's newest and most unusual art is underground. If you get time, go to one of the city's six underground **Metro bus-tunnel stations**.

Architects designed the roaring waterfall in Freeway Park to drown out the traffic on the freeway below. Almost 30,000 gallons of recycled water rush over the falls every minute.

Seattle Arts Commission (Artist: Richard Beyer)

Seattle-ites dress up and decorate *Waiting for the Interurban,* the city's favorite sculpture.

WHICH IS THE SAME?

Can you tell which two sculptures in the sculpture garden are exactly alike? When you've circled the sculptures that are the same, color in the scene.

FIRST HILL PLACES OF WORSHIP

First Hill is often called "Pill Hill" because many of Seattle's hospitals and doctor's offices are located here.

Five minutes from downtown, on First Hill, you can catch a glimpse of European culture in Seattle. That's where the wealthier settlers built their homes and churches.

Stained-glass windows as detailed as fine oil paintings line the walls of **Trinity Episcopal Church**, built in 1891. The building looks like an English country church. A German artist designed the windows.

Twin gold and white 175-foot towers make **St. James Cathedral** look like a palace from the outside. Inside and out, ornaments, curves, and scrolls, like icing on a birthday cake, decorate the cathedral. St. James, which was built in 1907, is a copy of the churches popular in Europe from 1550 to 1700.

Priteca, the architect who designed the **Temple de Hirsch Sinai** in 1960, said he wanted the Temple to look like a mountain. It does. It's very different from the ornate Paramount Theatre in downtown, which Priteca also designed.

Paul Otteson

Trinity Episcopal Church

Paul Otteson

Temple de Hirsch Sinai

DRAW YOUR OWN BUILDING

What would you build if you could build anything you wanted? In the space between the buildings, draw your ideal house, skyscraper, or office building. When you're done, color in the page.

SEATTLE CENTER

Seattle Center

Kids flying banners at the International Fountain

Gloria Bornstein

Gloria Bornstein calls her orcas sculpture *Neototems*.

In 1962, flags from all over the world flew on Seattle's World Fairgrounds. Today, wonderful and sometimes weird pieces of art decorate those same 74 acres, now renamed the **Seattle Center**.

To start a do-it-yourself-art-tour, walk through five archways shaped like castles, and buildings, and gates. The archways are really a painted steel sculpture called ***Endless Gate***. To see a sculpture that looks like it might blast off into space, continue along the path to the gigantic red ***Olympic Iliad***. Follow the music to the ***International Fountain***, a huge bowl-shaped fountain with a dome in the middle. A path spirals down into the center where jets of water shoot skyward like liquid fireworks. Two bronze sculptures of **orcas** swim in the grass next to the fountain. If you're wondering about the large bronze bell close to the fountain, it's a gift from Seattle's sister-city, Kobe, Japan. Give yourself time to explore the rest of the Center. There's lots more to see.

CONNECT THE DOTS

This landmark in downtown Seattle is the most recognizable in the Western U.S. Connect the dots to find out the identity of this mystery landmark, then color in the scene.

VIEWLAND-HOFFMAN ELECTRICAL SUBSTATION

Artist know what to do with old junk. If you'd like to know, too, then you and your parents should visit another of Seattle's best kept secrets, the Viewland-Hoffman Electrical Substation. The substation has been turned into a fantasy land by artists. Part of it is a moving, musical sculpture. Brightly painted windmills made from discarded coffee pots, dust pans, spoons, automobile parts, a toy duck, and much more, whir, creak, and hum. The electrical equipment is also painted in bright yellows, reds, and blues to show the path of electricity through the station. An unusual roofed cyclone fence that surrounds the substation looks like a sculpture itself.

When the Viewland-Hoffman substation was created, the city of Seattle asked artists and architects to work together to design both the building and the art.

Paul Otteson

Car parts were among the objects used to create this windmill.

Paul Otteson

The substation features brightly colored sculptures.

Without telling anyone what you're doing, ask for a word to fill in each blank. For example, "Give me an action word." When all the blanks are filled in, read the story out loud. One blank has been filled in for you.

Recycled Art!

When the kids went to the neighborhood garage sale, no one knew what they might find. They looked through the ___________ (describing word) piles of mushrooms (things) and found everything from garden tools to old toys. They decided to invent a ___________ (thing) out of the old junk. "Look!" said Dianna. "I can make ___________ (number) ___________ (things) out of these bottles and ___________ (things).

"___________ (exclamation)!" Chris said. "With this old golf club, we can invent a ___________ (thing) if the ___________ (animal) doesn't eat it first!" When they were done, the kids decided to start the first children's museum of ___________ (describing word) art.

At NOAA, you can read about the fierce white whale, Moby Dick. An artist used brass letters embedded in the two concrete footbridges to quote passages from Herman Melville's classic novel.

Paul Otteson

The *Sound Garden* at Magnuson Park

Paul Otteson

The Moby Dick Bridge at Magnuson Park

MAGNUSON PARK

Magnuson Park, a recycled U.S. Navy base, sprawls over 193 acres of open land at Sand Point on Lake Washington. This park is popular with swimmers, joggers, walkers, picnickers, kite fliers, and art lovers.

How would you like to listen to a sculpture? At Magnuson Park, you'll find one of Seattle's most unusual pieces of art. Just follow the path to the National Oceanographic and Atmospheric Administration's (NOAA) Regional Center and listen to the ***Sound Garden***. It's a pipe organ for the wind! Artist Douglas Hollis designed 12 steel towers of different heights, each with a vertical organ pipe. Part of the tower rotates toward the wind like a weather vane, and the wind plays through the pipes. Sit down on a bench and enjoy the concert.

MY TRAVEL JOURNAL

—Landmarks, Skyscrapers, and the Arts—

I had fun when I visited: ______________________________

I learned about: ______________________________

My favorite building was: ______________________________

What I enjoyed doing the most was: ______________________________

This is a picture of a building I saw

5 GOOD SPORTS

PEOPLE WHO LIVE IN SEATTLE LIKE TO BOAST that it's possible to sail in the morning, ski in the afternoon, and go to a basketball game in the evening. Seattle is a great place to play sports or to be a sports fan.

In Seattle, you can attend major league professional games in baseball, basketball, and hockey. The University of Washington Huskies have entertained football fans for 107 years. During SeaFair, a dozen hydroplanes race at 140 miles an hour on their Lake Washington course. Within an hour's drive of Seattle, you can watch professional bike and automobile racing.

If you're looking for sports activities within the city, you can swim, scuba dive, sail, kayak, play tennis, fish, golf, roller or ice skate, and hike. Just outside the city, you can horseback ride, ski, hike, mountain climb, or go hot-air ballooning or white-water rafting.

Keith W. Wood

Skiers find plenty of powder around Greater Seattle.

Reprinted with permission of University of Washington

Husky Stadium holds 72,500 "Dawgs" fans.

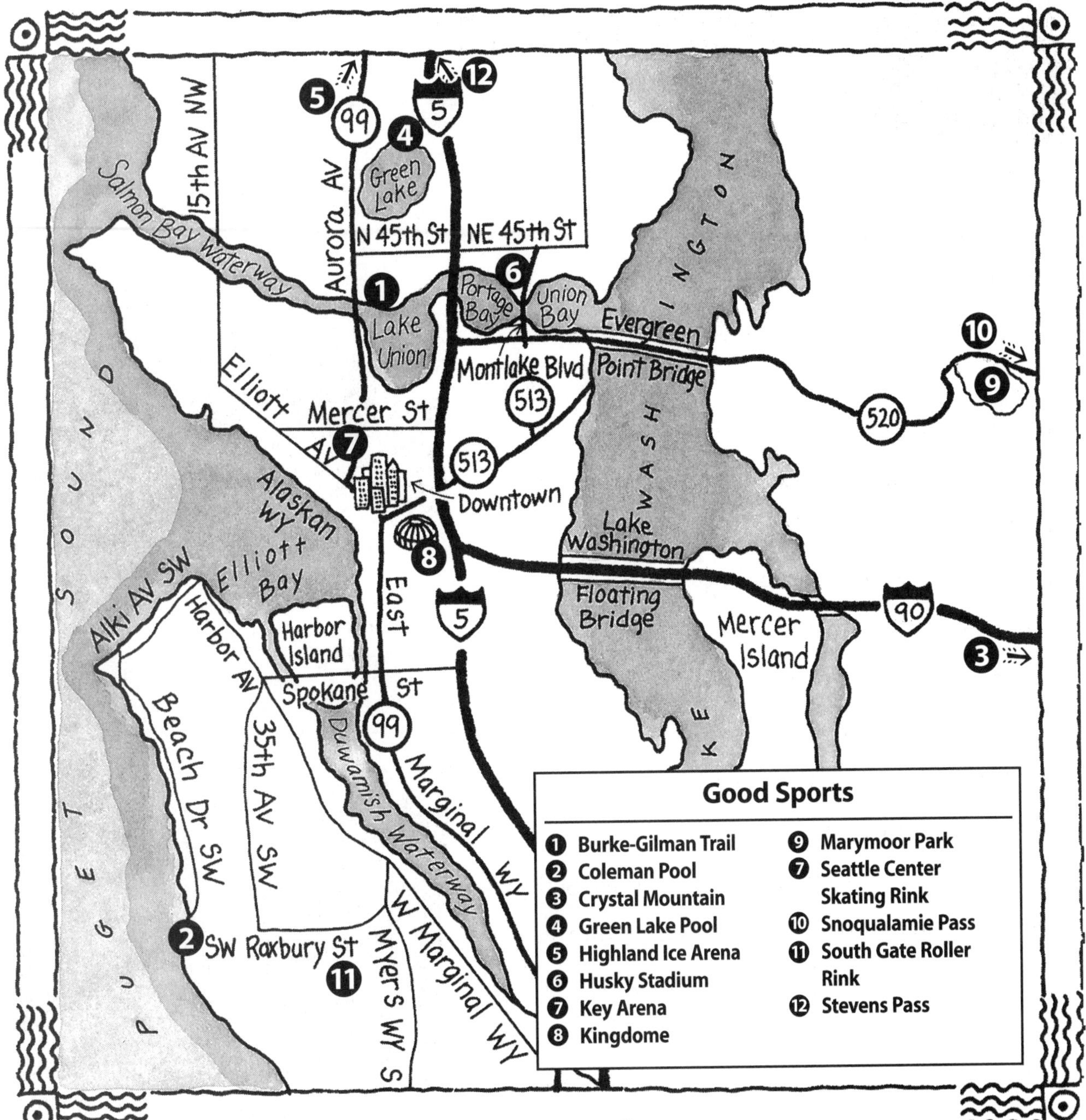

Good Sports
1 Burke-Gilman Trail
2 Coleman Pool
3 Crystal Mountain
4 Green Lake Pool
5 Highland Ice Arena
6 Husky Stadium
7 Key Arena
8 Kingdome
9 Marymoor Park
7 Seattle Center Skating Rink
10 Snoqualamie Pass
11 South Gate Roller Rink
12 Stevens Pass
Salmon Bay Waterway
15th AV NW
Aurora AV
Green Lake
N 45th St
NE 45th St
Portage Bay
Union Bay
Lake Union
Evergreen Point Bridge
Montlake Blvd
Elliott AV
Mercer St
Downtown
Alaskan WY
Elliott Bay
Alki AV SW
Harbor AV
Harbor Island
East Marginal WY
Spokane St
Lake Washington
Floating Bridge
Mercer Island
Beach Dr SW
35th AV SW
Duwamish Waterway
W Marginal WY
SW Roxbury St
Myers WY S
PUGET SOUND

SEATTLE SUPERSONICS

The basketball players race toward the basket. Shawn Kemp, forward for the SuperSonics, drives toward the basket and slam dunks the ball. "Another jam by The Rain Man," says fourth-grader Sam Grausz, as the cheers of the crowd fill the arena. The Sonics NBA games are fast-paced and intense. The Sonics know how to get their spot on the floor and hold it! "It's like jumping into a mosh pit with the American Gladiators," says Kemp.

During half-time entertainment, Big Foot, the team's mascot, will keep you smiling. From September through May, the Sonics play in the **Key Arena** at the Seattle Center. From the outside, the arena, with its swooping roof and giant concrete legs, looks like a Chinese pagoda. On the inside, every seat has a good view.

Jeff Reinking/NBA Photos

Gary Payton charges down the court.

Andy Hayt/NBA Photos

Sonics forward Shawn Kemp prepares to slam it.

The Seattle Thunderbirds play action-filled hockey at the Key Arena from September through March. ⇛

H. Conrad

Color to Find the Answer

What is orange and round and goes in a basket? Color all shapes with numbers in them orange. Color the shapes with letters in them any colors you want.

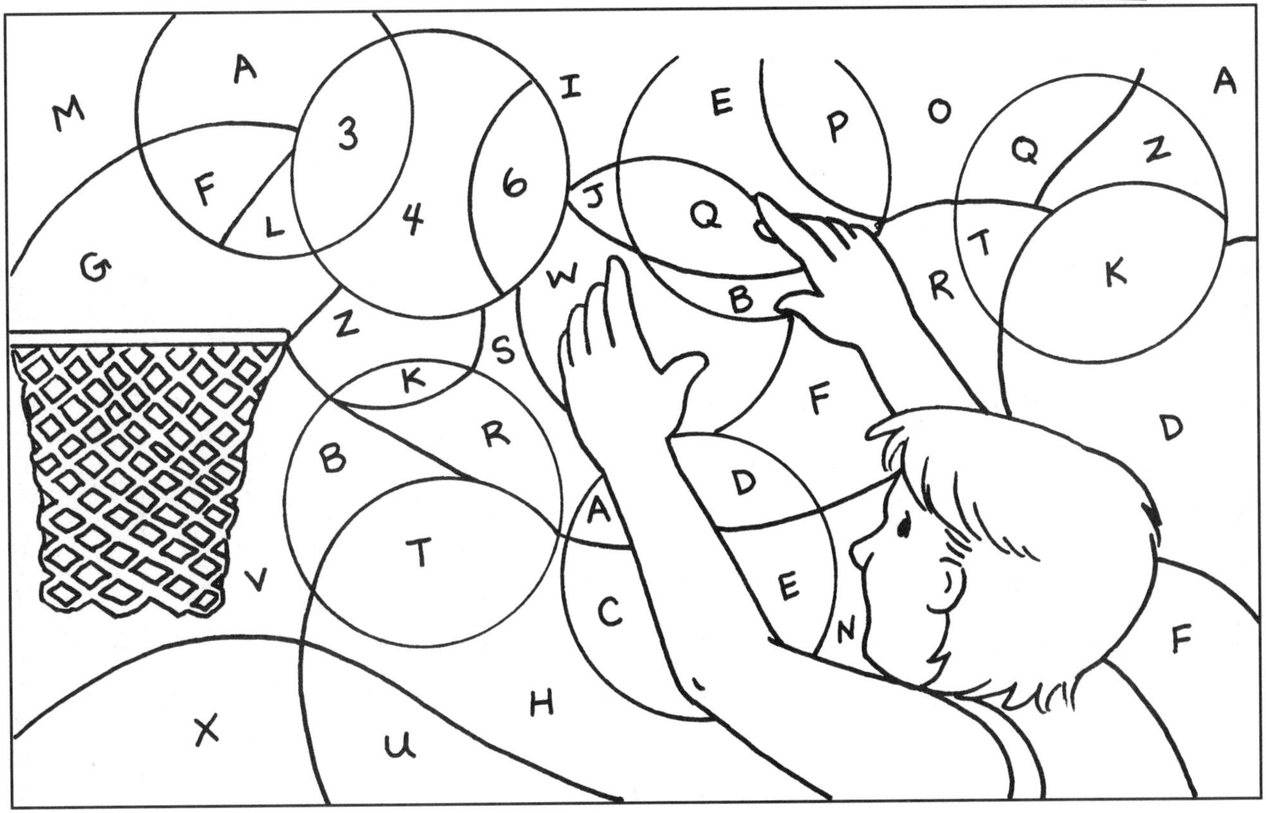

SEATTLE MARINERS

Professional baseball came to Seattle in 1938 with the Seattle Rainiers. Today, the Seattle Mariners play in the **Kingdome**. They hit grand slams, run double steals, and play the kind of baseball that took them to the 1995 American League playoffs. Mariners' pitcher Randy Johnson, also known as The Big Unit, can throw a ball 100 miles an hour. He received the Cy Young Award in 1995. Mariners' outfielder, Ken Griffey, Jr. has been on the All-Star team five times.

The Mariners play from April through early October. At various times throughout the season they give free bats, caps, or T-shirts to the first 2,000 kids to enter the Dome. Mariners' home runs are celebrated with a Kingdome fireworks display. Because of the Kingdome's closed roof, the crowd's cheers are the loudest in the league.

The Kingdome is 660 feet wide—big enough to tuck the Space Needle inside. The "Dome" seats 60,000 people for baseball, and even more for concerts.

Seattle Mariners

Pitcher Randy Johnson winds up for the pitch.

Mixed-up Picture Story

Help the Mariner's mascot put the scene in the correct order by filling in the number box in the bottom left-hand corner of each picture.

Seattle Mariners

UNIVERSITY OF WASHINGTON HUSKIES

Fast action and hard hitting make the Huskies (nicknamed the "Dawgs") exciting to watch. The Huskies are a PAC-10 Conference team and are often Rose Bowl contenders. Saturday home games are played September through November in **Husky Stadium**. It's the Northwest's largest outdoor stadium and holds 72,500 cheering fans.

The team's mascot, a husky dog, watches from the sidelines. The fancy footwork and lively music of the Husky Marching Band makes for great half-time entertainment. Cheerleaders guide you through cheers for "The Purple and the Gold."

Joanie Komura/Reprinted with permission of University of Washington

The Huskies are a PAC-10 Conference team.

Reprinted with permission of University of Washington

The Huskies marching band

You can enjoy Husky basketball November through March next door at Hec Edmundson Pavilion. The men's and the women's teams both play to big crowds, and you get a free bag of popcorn when you enter the pavilion.

FOOTBALL FEVER!

Hidden in this word search are some things you might find at a football game. Search for words vertically, horizontally, and diagonally. Can you find all 10 words? The first word has been found for you.

Word Box

grass	football
tackle	pass
cheerleader	referee
helmet	scoreboard
touchdown	fumble

Z C H E E R L E A D E R L F O
W F N A L K M E S O P A Y U G
E O H F R A H S Y M F E B M O
P O N L S G S E N R P T S B L
A T P O D R S S L B T O T L B
S B J E R S E Y R M E G N E I
S A T R M D A M G N E O G T J
D L S A G W N N H U I T Y E L
Q L F I C C T O U C H D O W N
O M Y J U K L E V A G R A S S
U I S E I S L R R E F E R E E
R O T B L K I E E U L I M Y K
S C O R E B O A R D I G B E T

Keith W. Wood

Riding the lift at Crystal Mountain Resort

Whether rain or shine, sleet or snow, Seattle sailors race their sailboats in a January event called the Frost-Bite Races.

SPORTS FOR YOU

Serious swimmers vote for the indoor pool at **Green Lake** and the outdoor **Coleman Pool** at **Lincoln Park**. Skiers from beginners to advanced head up to **Snoqualamie Pass**, **Stevens Pass**, or **Crystal Mountain**. Tennis players find courts scattered throughout the city. Soccer is also popular in Seattle.

If roller skating is your thing, try **South Gate Roller Rink**. For ice skating, check out **Highland Ice Arena**. From Thanksgiving to New Year's Day, you can glide across the ice at the **Seattle Center Skating Rink**.

Bikers, hikers, and in-line skaters can hit the trail at the **Burke-Gilman Trail**. It stretches out for 12 miles in Seattle, then continues on for a total of 25 miles, ending up in **Marymoor Park** in Redmond. Marymoor Park offers bike racing on a velodrome track. You can just watch, or you can join in if you're at least five feet tall.

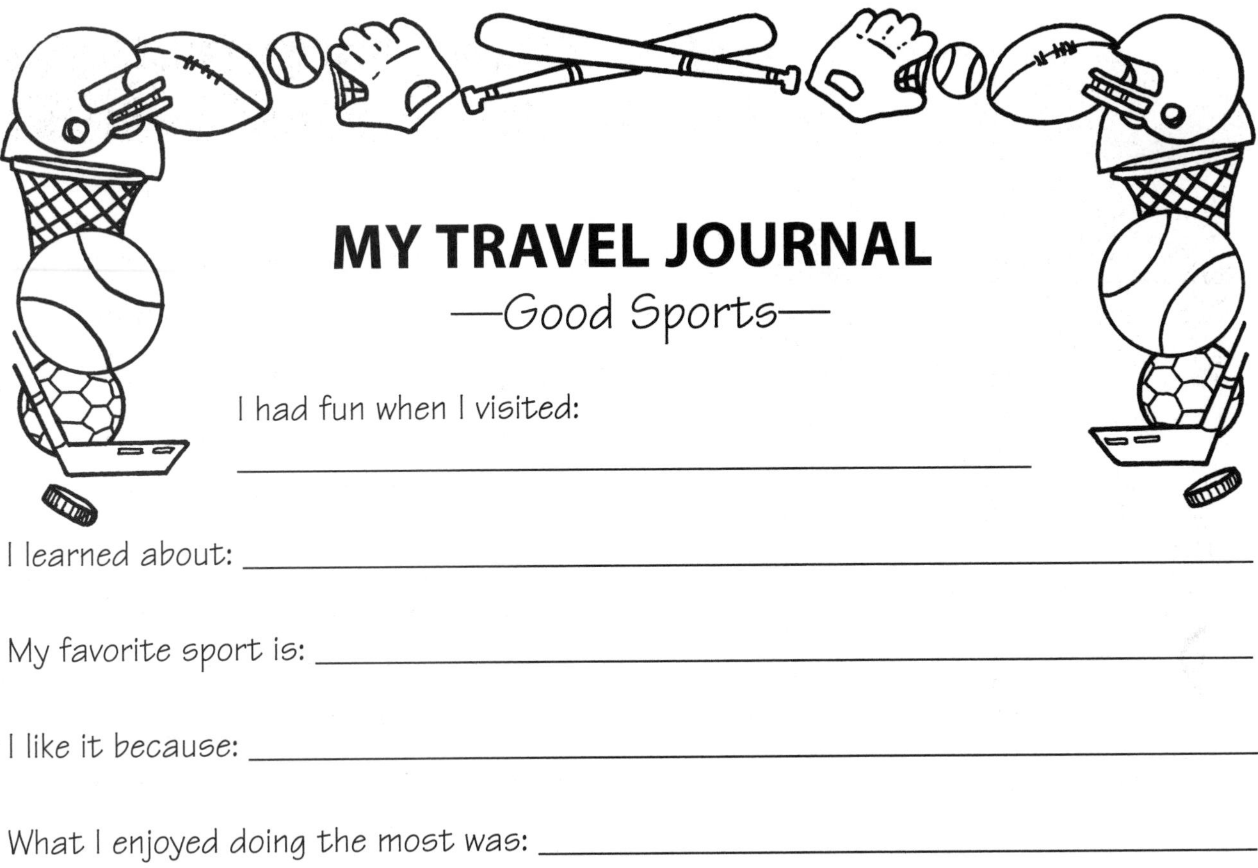

MY TRAVEL JOURNAL

—Good Sports—

I had fun when I visited: ______________________

I learned about: ______________________

My favorite sport is: ______________________

I like it because: ______________________

What I enjoyed doing the most was: ______________________

This is a picture of something I saw

MUSEUMS AND MORE

WHERE CAN YOU SEE A CASKET shaped like a car or thump a drum made by a Northwest Coast Native American? Where can you see works of art created hundreds of years before you were born? That's easy—at one of the 18 museums in Seattle. Whether you want to step back in time, explore the present, or leap into the future, there is a museum that is right for you. Most of them have discovery rooms or pull-out drawers where you can touch artifacts from displays. Often guides give museum tours. Some of the museums have computers and interactive CD-ROMs to make your tour even more fun. Other museums have displays that you can operate. Here are a few of the best museums you can explore.

A Tlingit raven rattle, on display at the Seattle Art Museum

Paul Macapia

The Pacific Science Center

Dennis Schatz

Museums and More

1. Museum of Flight
2. Museum of History and Industry
3. Nordic Heritage Museum
4. Pacific Science Center
5. Seattle Art Museum
6. Thomas Burke Museum
7. Wing Luke Asian Museum

SEATTLE ART MUSEUM

A 48-foot-tall mechanical sculpture named *Hammering Man* greets you at the front door of the Seattle Art Museum. Step inside the building, which is as beautiful as a piece of sculpture itself, and head for the grand staircase. You'll feel like you've entered a palace. Towering stone warriors and kneeling camels gaze at you from the stairs.

The museum galleries display traveling shows as well as a permanent collection of paintings and artifacts, such as the Tlingit bear war helmet and the delicately beaded octopus bag. In the **North Coast Native American Display**, you can wander among totem poles and masks arranged to make you feel a part of an ancient ceremony. You'll see scrolls, jade carvings, a tea house, and other artifacts from Japan, China, Korea, and India.

The African Collection includes a pink wood coffin from Ghana shaped like a luxury car. Allow time to watch videos and to explore the **Treasures from Around the World** drawers in the Educational Resource Room.

Seattle Arts Commission (Artist: Jonathan Borofsky)

Hammering Man guards the front door of the Seattle Art Museum.

CROSSWORD FUN

There is a lot to see at the Seattle Art Museum. Solve this crossword by figuring out the clues or completing the sentences. If you need help, use the clue box.

Clue Box

paint	sculpture
pottery	photographs
totem	museum
mask	brush

Across

1. When an artist carves a statue out of marble, she has made a __________.
4. With this stuff you can create a work of art or make your house a different color.
7. Clay plates, bowls, and cups are examples of this art form.
8. Unless you use your fingers, you need one of these before you paint!

Down

2. These are taken with a camera.
3. You wear one of these on Halloween.
5. This building can display everything from art to dinosaurs.
6. A __________ pole tells stories through carvings in wood.

WING LUKE ASIAN MUSEUM

This museum is tucked in among the shops in the **International District**, right next to Pioneer Square. Around 30,000 kids visit the Wing Luke Asian Museum each year to see artifacts, antiques, and photographs in a display called "One Song, Many Voices." The exhibit tells the story of the immigration and settlement of Asians and Pacific Islanders in Washington State over the past 200 years. Other displays explain silk making and how medicine is made from herbs.

After your stop at the museum, tour the International District where you'll see barbecued ducks hanging in restaurant windows, a fortune cookie factory, kung fu shops, and more. Take a trip down the giant spiral slide in the **International Children's Park** and pet the bronze dragon. Then trek over to **Uwajimaya**, a popular Asian supermarket and department store, where you'll find thousands of things from Asia, including tasty treats like dried squid and cow brains.

John Pai

Kids enjoy tours at the museum.

In the mood for an octopus dinner? Are you curious to try sushi or candy wrapped in edible paper? It's all at Uwajimaya Supermarket.

Without telling anyone what you're doing, ask for a word to fill in each blank. For example, "Give me an action word." When all the blanks are filled in, read the story out loud. One blank has been filled in for you.

Adventure in the International District

One day, while she was walking in the International District, ________ (girl's name 1) lost her ________ (thing 1). She was very ________ (emotion), because she had looked everywhere, but couldn't find it. She went into a scary (describing word) restaurant and asked the ________ (person or thing) for directions. With new directions, she walked until she came to ________ (place). She knew she would find it here.

She searched and searched, but she still couldn't find it. Suddenly, a woman with a ________ (thing) on her head stopped on the sidewalk to pick something up. It was ________ (girl's name 1)'s lost ________ (thing 1)! "________ (exclamation)!" said the girl. "You are a great help."

MUSEUM OF HISTORY AND INDUSTRY

The very glue pot that is believed to have started the Great Seattle Fire of 1889 sits in a case at the Museum of History and Industry. Here, everyday objects and artifacts, including a U.S. Mail airplane and a stuffed gorilla named Bobo, tell the history of Seattle.

Discover some of the things Seattle has given to the world, such as the electric guitar, water skis, Dick and Jane books, and the yellow happy face. Try on antique clothes or load a model of a modern containership in the **Hands-on-History** exhibit. You can walk through a full-sized model of an 1880 Seattle street and peek into a barber shop and other places. A large display on Smokey Bear is at the museum, too.

Museum of History & Industry, Seattle

Kids make pinwheels at the Museum of History and Industry.

Museum of History & Industry, Seattle/Howard Giske

An exhibit honored Smokey Bear's 50th birthday.

WHICH ARE THE SAME?

The term "flying saucer" was first used in Seattle in 1947. A pilot claimed to have spotted nine shining objects flying from Rainier toward Mount Adams. He said they looked like flying saucers with long waving tails.

Can you tell which two flying saucers are exactly alike? When you've circled the identical saucers, color in the scene.

THOMAS BURKE MUSEUM

If it's dinosaur skeletons you're interested in, the Thomas Burke Museum on the University of Washington campus is the place to go. Besides the different fossils on display, you can admire a huge stained-glass window by the world's most famous stained-glass designer, Louis Comfort Tiffany.

Other exhibits display artifacts from the Alaskan Arctic, the Pacific Rim, and the Northwest Coast, including a collection of large totem poles. Even the **Museum Cafe** is an artifact. Its wax pine walls were constructed in 1720 and once lined the walls of a French castle. The museum is named in honor of Judge Thomas Burke, who helped bring the Great Northern Railroad to Seattle.

After you've explored the museum, maybe you and your parents can take a look at the campus. If you enjoy buildings that look like castles, start with the **Suzzallo Graduate Library**.

If you're a night owl, a good place to watch the stars is from the University of Washington Observatory. It has a six-inch refractor telescope.

Mary Levin/University of Washington

The bones of this *Allosaurus* are about 140 million years old.

DRAW YOUR OWN TOTEM POLE

Here is a photo of a Tsimshian memorial totem pole on the right. Suquamish Indians carved certain animals on their totem poles to symbolize different members of their family. What animals would you choose?

Mary Levin

PACIFIC SCIENCE CENTER

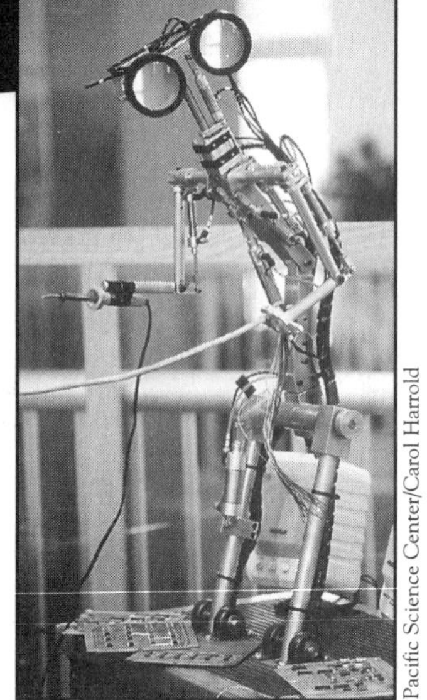

Max the Robot, resident of the Tech Zone at the Pacific Science Center

The Pacific Science Center is a science playground. Located in a cluster of six buildings on the Seattle Center grounds, it offers hundreds of fun things to do. You can operate robots, see what it's like to travel in a space capsule, or compose music in a computer lab.

Afterward, you can visit the **Tech Zone** and play virtual reality championship basketball. Test your strength—and your brain—on all sorts of devices, including the rock-climbing wall. Search the heavens in the **Planetarium** or catch a laser show. Slip into the **IMAX Theater** to watch a movie on a screen that's more than three stories high. Learn more about water power by playing with the water cannons, and play with other gadgets in the Science Center. All this thinking and playing will probably make you hungry, so you might want to stop by the **Science Center Cafe**.

Visitors operate a water cannon in the Water Works exhibit.

Thousands of ivy plants and hundreds of pounds of moss were used to make the life-sized dinosaurs on the lawn next to the Science Center.

CONNECT THE DOTS

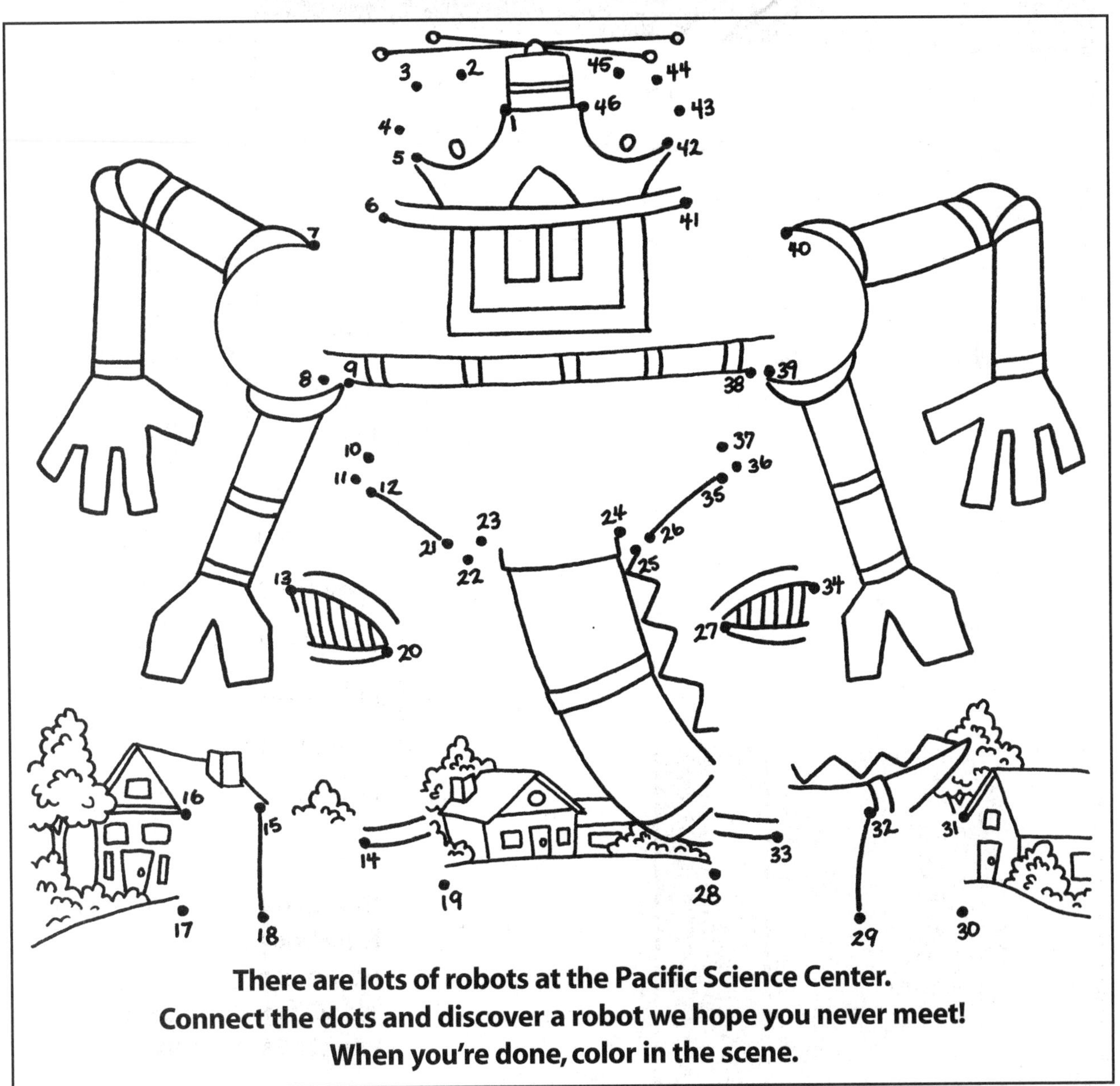

There are lots of robots at the Pacific Science Center. Connect the dots and discover a robot we hope you never meet! When you're done, color in the scene.

MUSEUM OF FLIGHT

Hungry? Try an authentic astronaut meal from the museum gift shop. There are freeze-dried ice-cream sandwiches, cheese pizzas, and complete chicken and rice dinners.

You can find all the important events in the history of flying at the Museum of Flight. Boeing's very first airplane manufacturing plant huddles next to the gigantic steel and glass **Great Gallery** crowded with historic airplanes. There's a replica of the Wright brothers' glider and the last remaining 1929 *Boeing 80*, a passenger plane.

You can see modern planes at the museum, too. Sit in a helicopter in the **Hangar Zone**, or check out an Apollo command module, a moon buggy, and a Russian unmanned space module. You can even work the controls of the U.S. Airforce *F-18*. The plane that steals the entire show is the Lockheed *M-12 Blackbird*, a U.S. spy plane. It can fly higher (16 miles up in the air) and faster than any other plane in the world.

Museum of Flight

Old and new aircraft are featured at the Museum of Flight.

WHAT'S MISSING?

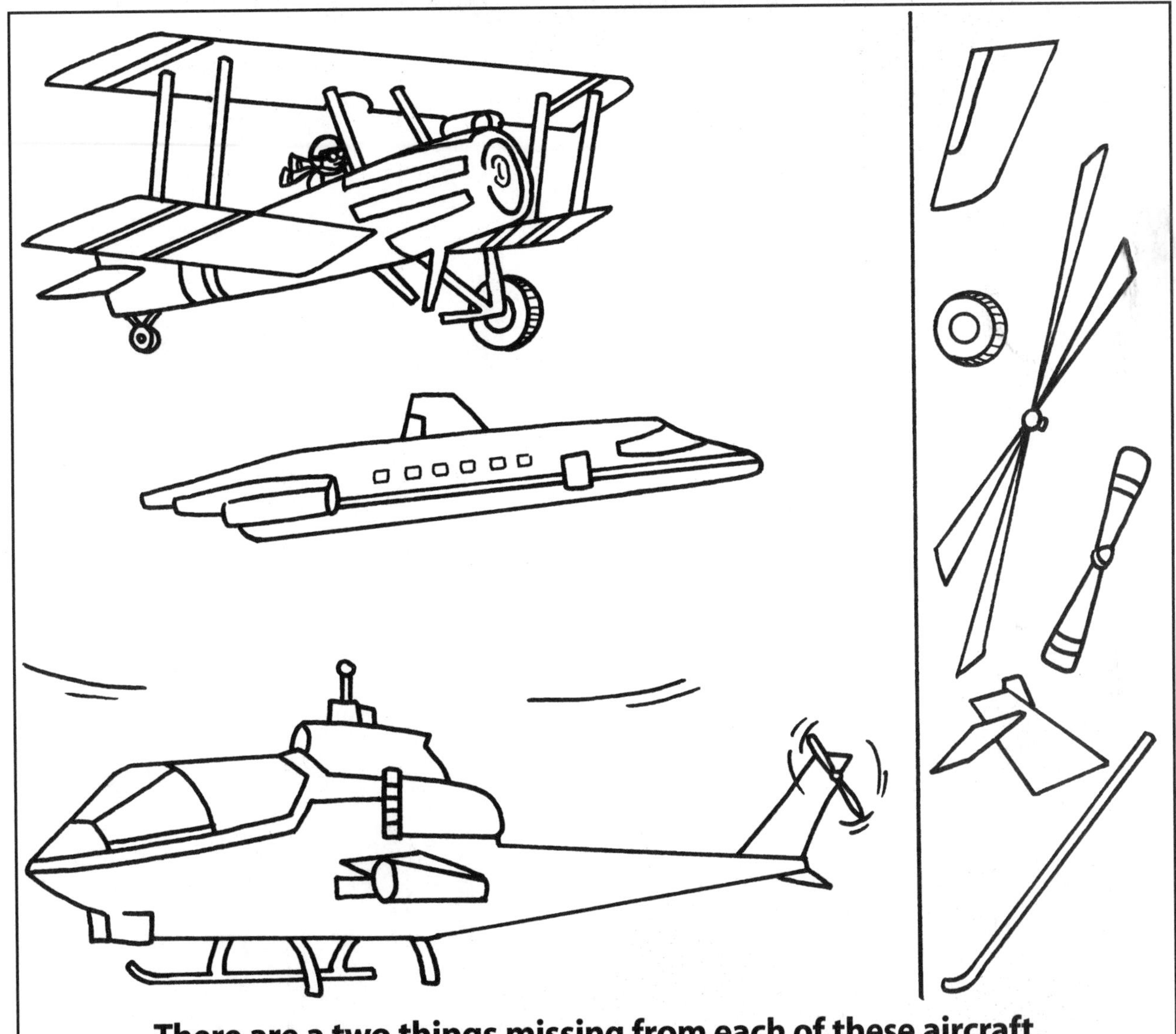

There are a two things missing from each of these aircraft. Draw lines from the missing parts to the craft that needs them.

NORDIC HERITAGE MUSEUM

At the Nordic Heritage Museum in Ballard, you can walk through exhibits that take you on a Scandinavian immigrant's journey from Europe to America. Peek into the window of a "room-barn" to see how a farm boy at the turn of the century lived in Sweden. Step aboard a ship bound for America, then walk down the gangplank at Ellis Island. Follow the immigrants through the slums of New York, then to the Midwest, and eventually to the Northwest and Ballard, where many of them settled.

Walk through a lumber camp, fish cannery, and a replica of the old town. Even the original door from the Ballard City Jail is at the museum. One room in the museum is devoted to Ivar Haglund, who built the Smith Tower.

In July, the museum celebrates Tivoli, a festival where you can taste many Scandinavian foods.

Nordic Heritage Museum

The Nordic Heritage Museum

Nordic Heritage Museum

Decorating a gingerbread house at the museum

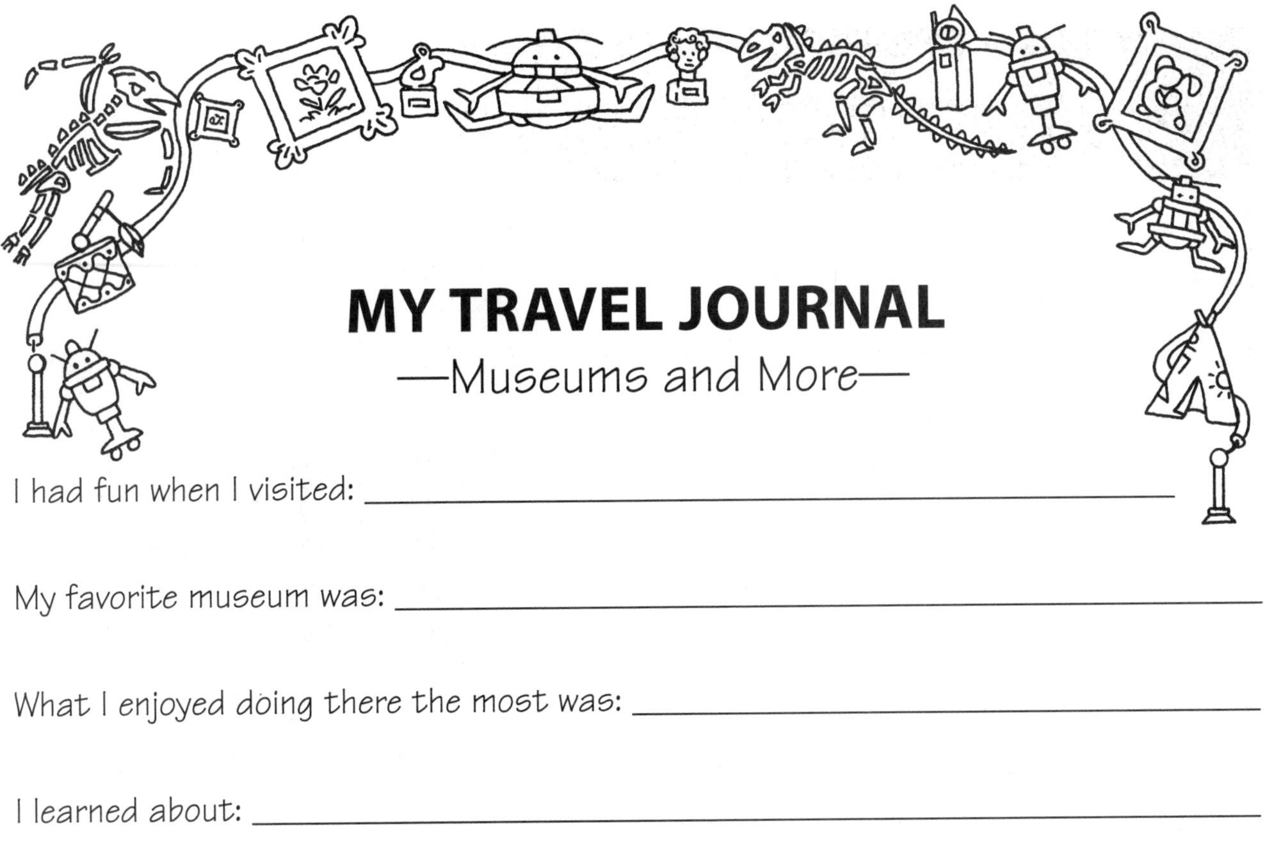

MY TRAVEL JOURNAL

—Museums and More—

I had fun when I visited: ______________________

My favorite museum was: ______________________

What I enjoyed doing there the most was: ______________________

I learned about: ______________________

This is a picture of a painting or sculpture I saw

7 THAT'S ENTERTAINMENT

IN BETWEEN YOUR SIGHTSEEING, WHY NOT take time out for a little entertainment? From bumper cars to water slides, from cool stores to a Native American Stage Show, you'll find hundreds of entertaining things in Seattle.

The Saturday edition of the *Seattle Times* lists entertainment activities for kids. So does *Seattle's Child*, a free monthly newspaper which can be found in libraries and bookstores. The daily *Seattle Times* includes movie listings for Seattle and the surrounding area.

Stop by the Visitor's Bureau at the Convention Center in downtown Seattle. The staff will fill you in on all the local entertainment. They also have hundreds of brochures about fun things to do and see. See the Resource Guide at the back of the book for important phone numbers.

Kevin Morris

The Tillicum Village Dancers

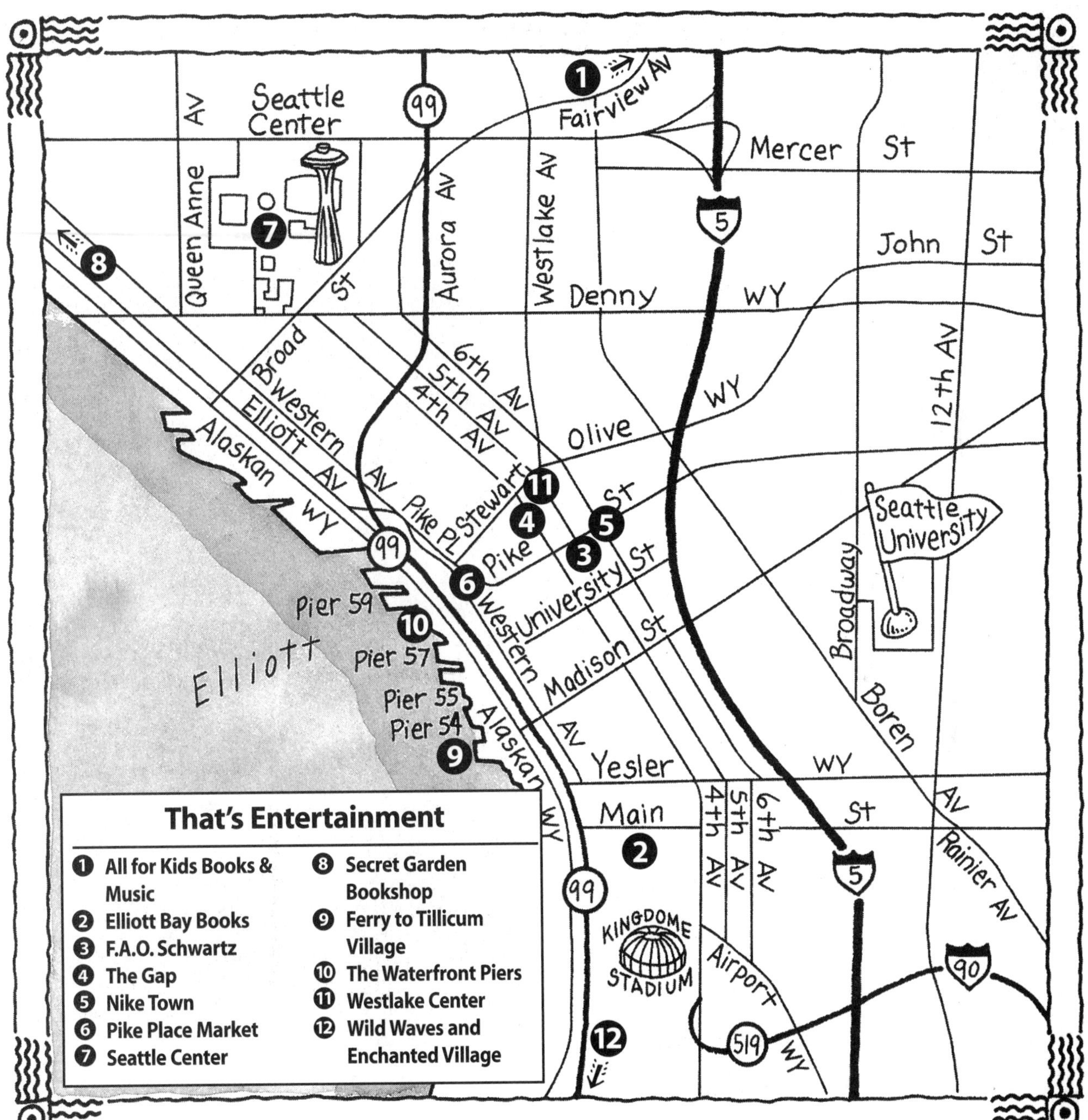

That's Entertainment
1 All for Kids Books & Music
2 Elliott Bay Books
3 F.A.O. Schwartz
4 The Gap
5 Nike Town
6 Pike Place Market
7 Seattle Center
8 Secret Garden Bookshop
9 Ferry to Tillicum Village
10 The Waterfront Piers
11 Westlake Center
12 Wild Waves and Enchanted Village
Seattle Center
Queen Anne Av
Aurora Av
Westlake Av
Fairview Av
Mercer St
John St
Denny WY
Broad St
Western Av
Elliott Av
Alaskan WY
6th Av
5th Av
4th Av
Olive WY
Stewart
Pike PL
Pike St
University St
Madison St
Yesler WY
Main St
Boren Av
Broadway
12th Av
Rainier Av
Airport WY
Seattle University
Pier 59
Pier 57
Pier 55
Pier 54
Elliott
Kingdome Stadium
99
5
90
519

THE WATERFRONT PIERS

Sylvester, an actual mummy of a gold rush prospector, awaits you at **Ye Olde Curiosity Shop** on Pier 54. You'll also find shrunken heads and a grain of rice with the Lord's Prayer written on it. On Pier 55, you can buy beautiful polished stones, 13 kinds of fudge, and, at The Frankfurter, the best hot dogs in town.

At the **Bay Pavilion** on Pier 57, you can play virtual reality games at the Big Top Arcade. There are also souvenir shops, an indoor carousel, and a famous sourdough bread bakery.

On Pier 59 at the **Omnidome**, a theater with a 180-degree dome movie screen, you'll soar into the volcanic crater at Mount St. Helens in a helicopter. You'll feel like you're part of the action.

Seattle's piers are built diagonally to the land rather than straight out. Because there aren't any sharp turns, it's easier for boats to dock.

Omnidome/Graphics Film

↑ *The Eruption of Mount St. Helens* plays regularly at the Omindome.

← The Omnidome is on Pier 59 in Waterfront Park

Omnidome Film Experience/ Jerry Wade

COLOR THE SCENE

A ferry leaves from one of Seattle's piers to explore Elliot Bay. Color the scene.

Pike Place Market PDA

More than 100 farmers sell fresh fruits and vegetables at the Market.

PIKE PLACE MARKET

Climb up 72 stairs from the waterfront and you'll see grown-ups throwing fish at one another. It happens in the fishmonger's stall at the Pike Place Market. Nine million people visit the market each year. It's noisy, crowded, and lots of fun. In business since 1907, the market is built on three levels and is several blocks long. *Rachel the Pig*, a fat, bronze, bigger-than-life piggy bank, greets you at the market's entrance. Rachel likes to be fed!

Move through the market to see piles of fresh fruits and vegetables. Flowers, foods, and crafts are all sold at the market. If you need a kite, comic book, baseball cards, funky clothes, souvenirs, a wind-up toy, a new magic trick, or almost anything else, be sure to come here.

Pike Place Market PDA

The fish stalls at the Market sell fresh salmon, shellfish, and other fish.

John Stamets

***Rachel the Pig* gobbles about $9,000 each year. The money is used to help support the Market Foundation, which provides helpful services to neighborhood residents.**

Without telling anyone what you're doing, ask for a word to fill in each blank. For example, "Give me an action word." When all the blanks are filled in, read the story out loud. One of the blanks has been filled in for you.

Rachel the Pig Escapes!

Everyone at Pike Place Market knew that Rachel the Pig was a ________ (describing word) bronze piggy bank. But one day, a magic ________ (person) arrived in Seattle. He waved his ________ (thing) over the piggy bank and suddenly Rachel began to fly (action word). "I'm so ________ (describing word)," said Rachel. "I think I'll go play around ________ (place)." Rachel ________ (action word) through the market, where she ate every ________ (thing) she saw. "I'm one very tired ________ (thing)," she squealed to herself. So she trotted back to her ________ (place) and went to sleep.

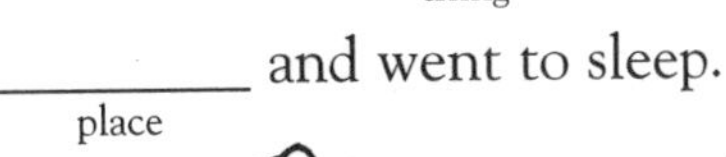

DOWNTOWN RETAIL STORES

If you've saved up your allowance and have money to spend, you'll find terrific stores in downtown Seattle. At **F.A.O. Schwartz**, one of the world's most popular toy stores, you can play a tune by strolling across a piano-key bridge. While you check out the store's toys, games, and other fun things, a stuffed dinosaur talks to you. You might want to have your picture taken with the humongous bronze teddy bear in front of the store.

If you're a sports fan, head over to **Nike Town**. If you want cool clothes for school, stop by **The Gap**. If the skies are drippy and you and your family aren't in the mood to dodge raindrops, slip into **Westlake Center**. It's a four-story shopping mall with all kinds of stores, including one shop which sells only products made in Washington.

Seattle–King Co. News Bureau

Westlake Center

Downtown Seattle has more street clocks than any other city in the U.S. Some clocks are antique, some are modern, and some are just plain weird, like the leaning clock at Third Avenue and University Street.

WHICH ARE THE SAME?

Can you tell which two clocks are exactly alike?
When you've circled the identical clocks, color in the scene.

BOOKSTORES FOR KIDS

Is your brain on overload from sightseeing? Are your feet sore? It might be time to curl up with a good book. Seattle has more than 130 bookstores that sell new books and 70 more that sell used books. **Elliott Bay Books** in Pioneer Square stocks over 125,000 titles and has an entire room for kid's books. On Saturdays, the store sponsors storytellers.

Seattle also has two bookstores just for kids: the **Secret Garden Children's Bookshop** in the Ballard District and **All for Kid's Books and Music** in Northeast Seattle. Authors and illustrators come to these stores to do book signings and readings. Call ahead to find out if anyone will be in town when you're in Seattle.

Maurice Sendak, author of *Where The Wild Things Are*, designed the sets for the Pacific Northwest Ballet's *Nutcracker*, which is performed every December at the Opera House in the Seattle Center.

A. Kachaturian/Archive Photos

Maurice Sendak with his wild friends

WHOSE BOOK IS IT?

Draw a line connecting the book on the shelf with the kid you think would like it the most. For example, a girl walking a dog would enjoy a book about dogs.

SEATTLE CENTER

From downtown you can zip out to the Seattle Center on the **Monorail**, a 90-second, up-in-the-air ride. At the center, you'll step off the Monorail and into the **Fun Forest**, an amusement park with bumper-cars, a merry-go-round, and the Bonanza Shooting Gallery.

At nearby **Center House**, you'll find the **Children's Museum, Seattle Fudge**, fast-food places, and dozens of shops. If you enjoy skateboarding, watch the action in **Skateboard Park**. If you like a challenge, join the crowd at the **International Fountain** and try to outrun its acrobatic water jets. A nice way to top off a visit is to attend a play at the **Charlotte Martin Children's Theater**. The theater building is tiled in fanciful colors making it look like a tapestry.

Seattle Center

The Monorail whisks passengers downtown in 90 seconds.

Thirty years ago, the movie *It Happened at the World's Fair* was filmed at Seattle Center, with Elvis Presley as the leading man.

Seattle Center

The Wind Storm roller coaster, in the Fun Forest Amusement area

WHAT'S WRONG HERE?

Name at least 10 things that you think are wrong in this picture. Circle them when you find them, then color the scene.

TILLICUM VILLAGE

Kevin Morris

Cooking salmon the traditional way

An eight-mile boat trip from downtown Seattle puts you on tiny **Blake Island**, a former Suquamish fishing camp and the birthplace of Chief Sealth. With clam shells crunching under your feet, you can walk the same beach Chief Sealth once walked. If you and your parents are hungry, you can enjoy a salmon dinner in the Tillicum Village **Longhouse**. Salmon is cooked on cedar stakes over alderwood fires by Native American chefs who prepare the fish the way their ancestors did. After dinner, you'll be entertained with a celebration of Northwest Coast Native American songs, dances, and legends.

Kevin Morris

The Tillicum Longhouse

Blake Island and Tillicum Village are now part of a 500-acre state park that includes forests and beaches. Before the tour boat whisks you back to Seattle, take time to explore the island. The Tillicum Village trip, which includes dinner, entertainment, and a tour of Seattle's harbor, takes about four hours.

A TRIP TO TILLICUM

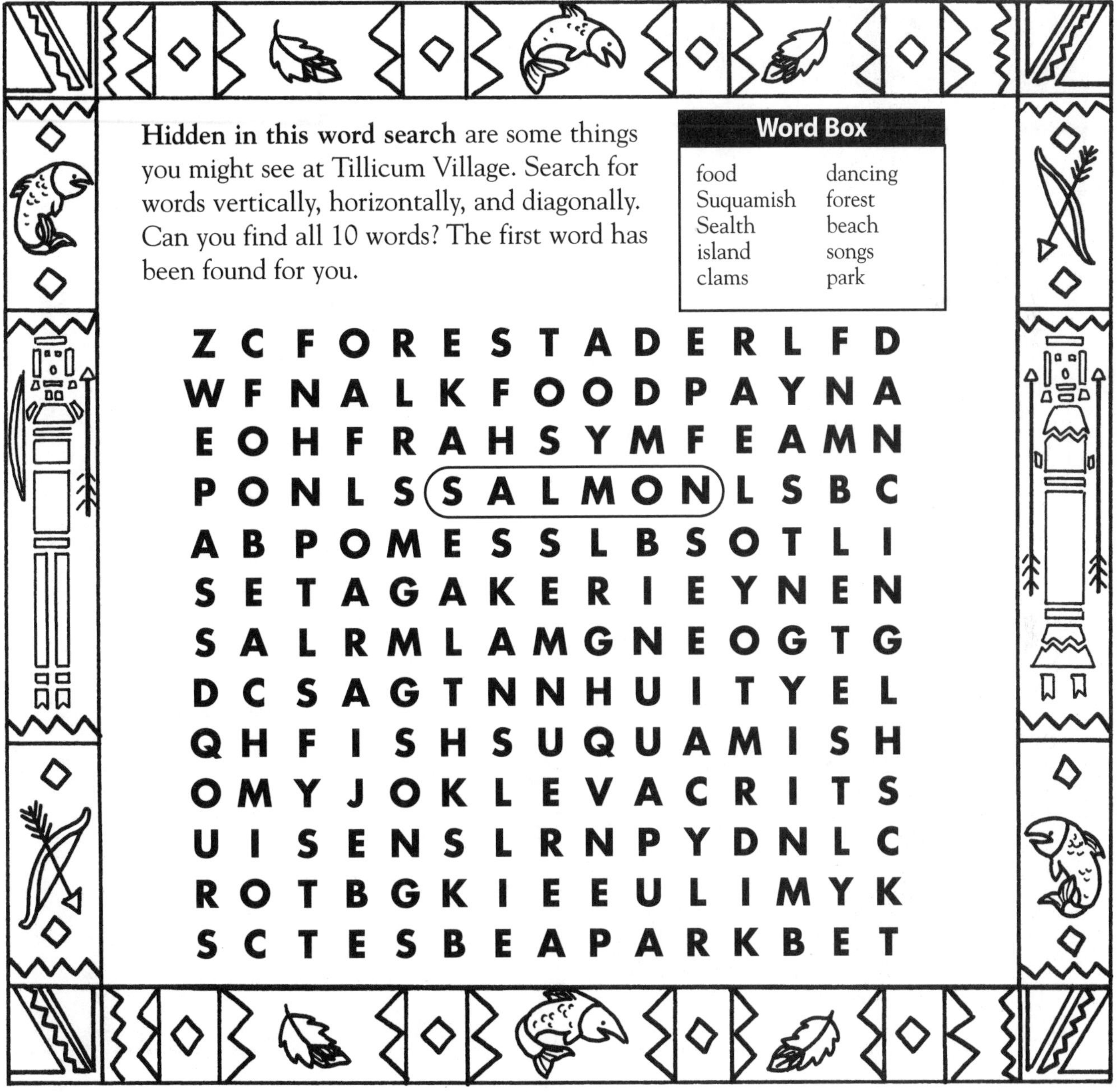

Hidden in this word search are some things you might see at Tillicum Village. Search for words vertically, horizontally, and diagonally. Can you find all 10 words? The first word has been found for you.

Word Box

food	dancing
Suquamish	forest
Sealth	beach
island	songs
clams	park

```
Z C F O R E S T A D E R L F D
W F N A L K F O O D P A Y N A
E O H F R A H S Y M F E A M N
P O N L S S A L M O N L S B C
A B P O M E S S L B S O T L I
S E T A G A K E R I E Y N E N
S A L R M L A M G N E O G T G
D C S A G T N N H U I T Y E L
Q H F I S H S U Q U A M I S H
O M Y J O K L E V A C R I T S
U I S E N S L R N P Y D N L C
R O T B G K I E E U L I M Y K
S C T E S B E A P A R K B E T
```

WILD WAVES AND ENCHANTED VILLAGE

Enchanted Village is an amusement park the size of 20 city blocks that includes rides, bumper boats, an antique doll and toy museum, a wading pool, and a small zoo.

Next door is Wild Waves, the largest water park in the Northwest. You'll go a little wild as you enjoy the park's watery rides. For starters, try the water slides, the gigantic wave pool, and inner tube rides.

The park is in the town of **Federal Way** about 45 minutes south of Seattle. Plan to spend the day there to make the trip worthwhile. There are food concessions in the Enchanted Village, but many families prefer to pack a picnic lunch.

For a thrilling ride that doesn't cost a penny, take a trip on the longest and steepest escalator west of the Mississippi. The escalator is located in the Pioneer Square Bus Tunnel Station at Third Avenue and Yesler Way.

Wild Waves

Enjoying the water at Wild Waves

Enchanted Village

Kids enjoy the rides at Enchanted Village.

MY TRAVEL JOURNAL

—That's Entertainment—

These are the names of the places I visited: ______________________________

My favorite place was: ______________________________

What I enjoyed doing the most was: ______________________________

The strangest thing I saw was: ______________________________

This is a picture of something I saw

8 LET'S EAT!

FROM THE LEMONADE AND HOT DOG STANDS on the sandy sidewalks at Alki Beach, to the fancy revolving dining room at the top of the Space Needle, Seattle has lots of places that welcome kids and have tasty food. If you and your family are eager to try foods from other countries, there are many restaurants that serve all sorts of ethnic foods: Chinese, Japanese, Thai, Greek, Italian, Scandinavian, Mexican, and Indonesian, to name a few.

Pike Place Market PDA

You can find the freshest ingredients at Pike Place Market.

If you're looking for inexpensive meals, tell your family to stop by a Seattle supermarket and put together a picnic. Many of the markets—Larry's Market across from the Seattle Center for one—also have delis or salad bars. Slip your meal into your backpack and head for a park.

Bruce Hilliard

At the Old Spaghetti Factory, you can dine in an old caboose.

Let's Eat
1 Chinook's
2 Cucina! Cucina!
3 The Garden Court
4 Iron Horse Restaurant
5 Ivar's Acres of Clams and Fish Bar
6 Ivar's Salmon House
7 The Market Cafe
8 Ocean City
9 Old Spaghetti Factory
10 Pacific Picnic
11 Three Girls Bakery
Seattle Center
Queen Anne AV
Aurora AV
Westlake AV
Fairview AV
Mercer St
John St
Denny WY
Broad St
Western AV
Elliott AV
Alaskan WY
6th AV
5th AV
4th AV
Olive WY
Stewart
Pike PL
Pike St
University St
Madison St
Yesler WY
Main St
4th AV
5th AV
6th AV
Broadway
12th AV
Boren AV
Rainier AV
Seattle University
Pier 59
Pier 57
Pier 55
Pier 54
Bay
Kingdome Stadium
Airport WY
99
5
90
519

FISHY FACTS

Even if you think you only like hamburgers, you'll enjoy eating at Seattle's seafood restaurants. The fish is as fresh and delicious as any you will ever have. In fact, the restaurants are often next door to the boats that brought in the fish.

Ivar's Acres of Clams and Fish Bar on the Seattle waterfront is famous for its clam nectar, clam chowder, and fish and chips. The restaurant serves full meals, including hamburgers. Be sure to notice Seattle's two fire boats moored next door at Pier 56. **Ivar's Salmon House** on Lake Union is another favorite. The salmon dinner includes mouth-watering corn bread and place mats that double as Indian masks.

Another fish restaurant that's fun to go to is **Chinook's** at Fisherman's Terminal on Salmon Bay. Besides great fish, Chinook's serves pasta, grilled cheese sandwiches, and burgers. Their wild mountain blackberry cobbler will put you in orbit.

Fisherman's Terminal is home base to more than 700 fishing boats. This is one of the largest commercial fishing fleets in the world.

WHAT'S THE DIFFERENCE?

These two pictures might look the same, but they are not. How many differences between the two scenes can you find? Hint: There are at least 15 differences.

THE TASTE OF SEATTLE

Ocean City is a big, bright Chinese restaurant in the International District that serves lots of different meat and vegetable dishes. Nicknamed "Noodle City" by the locals, Ocean City serves dim sum, a buffet cart that offers lots of tasty Chinese foods that are very hard to pronounce.

Cucina! Cucina! on Lake Union offers delicious pizzas baked in wood-burning ovens. The restaurant also serves salads, lasagna, and other pasta dishes. Chefs give you your own pizza dough to sculpt, then they bake your creations!

If you're in a hurry and nobody in your family can make up their minds where to eat, an inexpensive choice is **Pacific Picnic**. Located on the third floor of Westlake Center in downtown Seattle, Pacific Picnic is a carnival of ethnic and American foods. They serve everything from soup in a scooped-out loaf of sourdough bread, to corn tacos covered in spicy salsa. The Monorail Terminal is on the third floor, too.

The Seattle phone book lists 139 delicatessens and too many restaurants to count.

Cucina! Cucina! Inc.

Cucina! Charlie dances at the opening of Cucina! Presto.

FIND THE FOOD

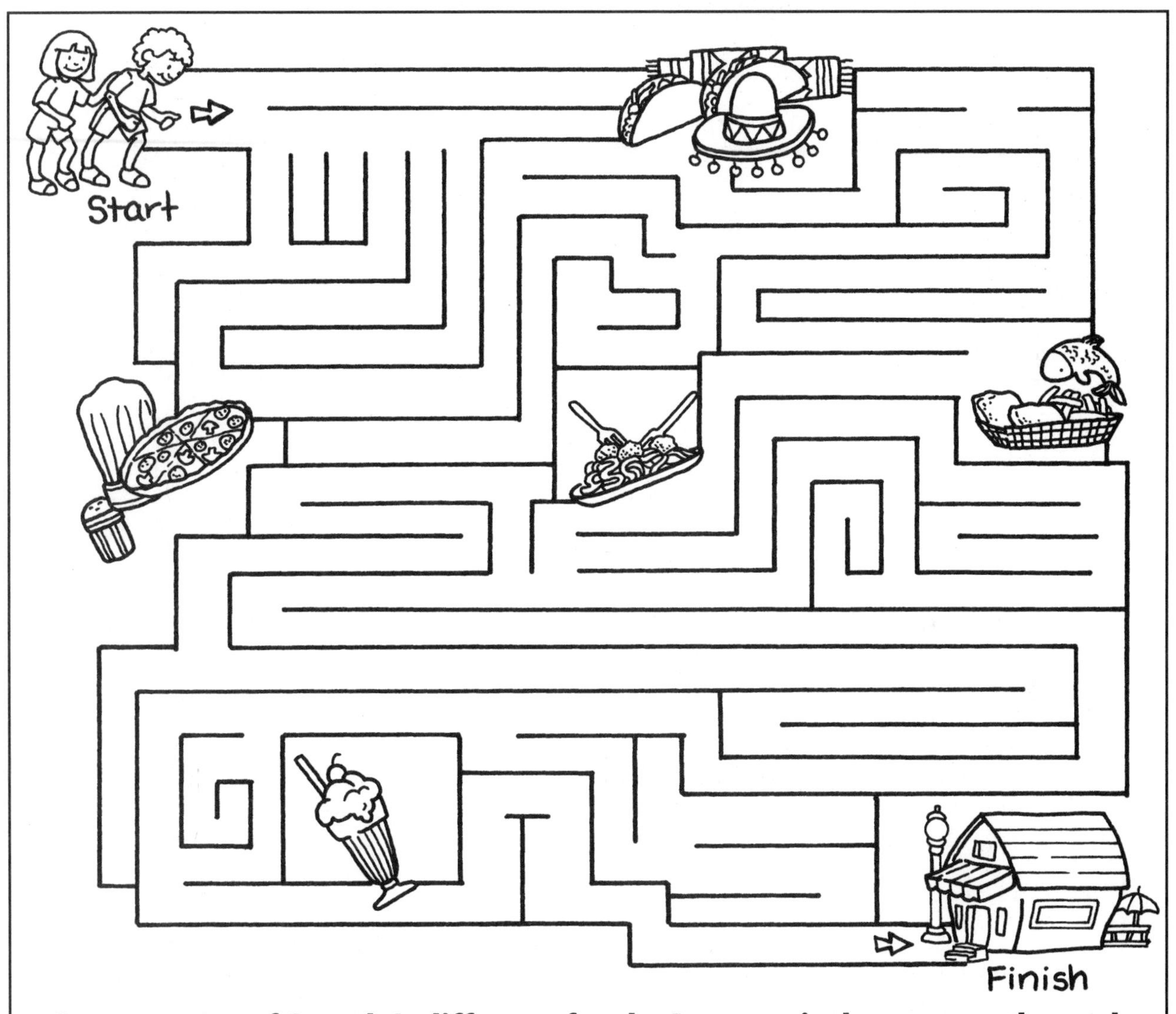

Go on a tour of Seattle's different foods. As you wind your way through the maze, see if you can collect every kind of food in the maze.

THE WEIRD AND THE WONDERFUL

At the **Iron Horse** restaurant, you can order a buffalo burger, a chocolate peanut butter milk shake, and a giant salad and have it all delivered to your table by an electric train that whistles. Train posters and pictures, model trains, and bits and pieces from real trains cover the restaurant walls. The menu includes sandwiches, burgers (beef and buffalo), chicken, tacos, floats, and lots of good desserts. Prices are reasonable for both lunch and dinner.

Absolutely everybody goes to the weird and wonderful **Old Spaghetti Factory**. There you can eat while sitting on an ancient bedstead or in a caboose parked in the middle of the room. Don't forget to weigh yourself on the huge scale before and after you eat. The restaurant serves spaghetti with every imaginable topping. They also serve salads, chicken, and Italian ice cream.

If you're in the mood for sandwiches, baked goods, and hearty soups, try **Three Girls Bakery** in the Sanitary Market at the Pike Place Market. It's a lunch counter that also has a takeout window.

CROSSWORD FUN

Solve this crossword by figuring out the clues or completing the sentences. If you need help, use the clue box.

Across

1. Many people eat tartar sauce with their ______ and chips.
5. Ice______ is many people's favorite dessert.
6. If it's a hot day, try a milk______ with a cherry on top.
8. If you go out to dinner, this is where you will eat.

Down

2. You don't have to be Italian to enjoy this pasta dish.
3. If you have a sweet tooth, you might eat this after dinner.
4. There's no ham in this food, but people still call it a ham______.
7. You might need dressing for this leafy dish.
9. Clam chowder is this type of food.

Clue Box

burger
dessert
cream
shake
restaurant
spaghetti
fish
salad
soup

GREAT HOTEL EATS

A glass counter crammed with pies, cakes, and all sorts of goodies is the first thing you see as you walk into the **Market Café** at the **Westin Hotel**. The restaurant is decorated with pots of flowers, pictures of the Pike Place Market, and a replica of the Pergola—the fancy iron and glass building in Pioneer Square that once served as a shelter for trolley passengers. The Market Café has a long menu that includes vegetarian dishes. The waiters even give you crayons to draw with while you wait for your meal.

If you and your family are in the mood to treat yourselves to an unforgettable experience, you might want to visit the **Garden Court** at the **Olympic Four Season's Hotel**. Every Sunday, a Winnie-the-Pooh brunch lets you watch Pooh videos while you eat. In the spring and summer, there is also a Children's Tea that serves fruit breads, scones with Devonshire cream, snowberry jam, and pots of steaming tea.

During the Christmas holidays, the Olympic Four Seasons transforms several elegant rooms into the Teddy Bear Suite. Ask for the key at the desk and drop in (no charge) to chat with the bears, munch gingerbread cookies, and sit in front of the fire.

Kevin Morris

The Teddy Bear Suite

MY TRAVEL JOURNAL

—Let's Eat!—

These are the names of some of the restaurants I ate at:

____

My favorite restaurant was: ______________________

The food I enjoyed there the most was: ______________

The most unusual food I ate was: ________________

Mt least favorite food was: ____________________

This is a picture of one restaurant I visited

CALENDAR OF SEATTLE EVENTS

January

Chinese New Year

Children's Museum, (206) 441-1768
Wing Luke Asian Museum, (206) 623-5124

Kids and Critters Naturefest

Northwest Trek, (800) 433-8735
In mid-January, the Northwest Trek Wildlife Park sponsors activities to help kids learn about the animals in the park.

Martin Luther King Jr. Day

Seattle Center House, (206) 684-7200

February

February Festival

Langston Hughes Cultural Center, (206) 684-4757
African American culture and history are celebrated with talent shows, plays, exhibits, and musical performances.

Festival Sundiata

Seattle Center, (206) 684-7200
Talent shows, plays, exhibits, and musical performances help celebrate African and African American history and culture.

Imagination Celebration

Seattle Center, (206) 441-4501
This is a week-long celebration of the arts. It includes performances, hands-on activities, student displays, and other events designed to let kids explore the arts.

Northgate Children's Fair

Northgate Mall, (206) 362-4777

Smile Day

Seattle Aquarium, (206) 443-7607
This one-day event, designed to promote good dental care, features activities, goodies, guest appearances, and free dental screenings for kids under age 12.

March

St. Patrick's Day Parade

Seattle, (206) 623-0340

Whirligig

Seattle Center House, (206) 684-7200
This month-long carnival is held indoors at the Seattle Center. It includes amusement park rides, entertainment, and performances for kids.

Japanese Cultural and Cherry Blossom Festival

Seattle Center, (206) 684-7200

April

Daffodil Festival

Puyallup, (206) 627-6176.
This festival celebrates Washington's daffodils.

Kid's Fun Fair
Seattle's Kingdome, (206) 441-1881
Held at the Kingdome, this fair has lots of kids' activities as well as helpful information for parents.

Skagit Valley Tulip Festival
Mt. Vernon, (360) 428-8547

May

Parade of Boats
Seattle, (206) 623-0340
At 10 a.m. on the first Saturday of May, crew races are held on the Montlake Cut. The races are followed at noon by a parade of decorated pleasure boats.

Marie Mills/David Cummings/Unicorn Stock Photos

The Gentlemen Jugglers perform at the Northwest Folklife Festival.

Northwest Folklife Festival
Seattle Center, (206) 684-7300
This Memorial Day Weekend festival includes the International Children's Village, which has stage performances, workshops, and hands-on activities.

Norwegian Constitution Day
Seattle, (206) 543-0645

Pike Place Market Festival
Seattle, (206) 587-0351
Also held on Memorial Day weekend, this festival has entertainment and hands-on activities for kids and their parents. Kids' Alley is a special feature at the festival. Call ahead for special events and activities.

International Children's Festival
Seattle Center, (206) 684-7346
For an entire week, performers from around the world—puppeteers, actors, dancers, musicians, storytellers, and others—entertain kids. Children from dozens of countries attend as well.

University District Street Festival
Seattle, (206) 527-2567

International Children's Film Festival
Children's Museum, Seattle Center, (206) 441-1768

June

Seattle Fire Festival
Pioneer Square, (206) 622-6235
This Pioneer Square festival includes a display of antique fire trucks, entertainment, kids activities, fire department demonstrations, and displays that tell the story of the Great Seattle Fire of 1889.

Freemont District Street Fair
Seattle, (206) 633-4409

Greek Festival
Seattle, (206) 323-8557

Heritage and Strawberry Festival
Burien, (206) 241-4647
This Burien festival celebrates summer with arts and crafts, entertainment, performances, food booths, and mountains of strawberries and shortcake.

Philippine Festival
Seattle, (206) 684-7200

July

Bon Odori
Seattle, (206) 329-0800
This Japanese summer dance festival is sponsored by the Seattle Buddhist Temple. It is held in the International District. The two-day festival includes street dancing, drumming, and food booths for the whole family.

Flight Festival and Air Show
Seattle, (206) 764-5720

AT&T and Cellular One's Family Fourth
Seattle, (206) 281-7788
The Fourth of July celebration at Gas Works Park features a fireworks display on Lake Union.

Ivar's Fireworks Celebration
Seattle, (206) 587-6500

Lake Union Wooden Boat Festival
Seattle, (206) 382-2628

Kid's Fair/Bellevue Arts and Crafts Fair
(206) 454-4900

Paine Field International Air Fair
Everett, (206) 355-2266

SeaFair

SeaFair is one of Seattle's most popular festivals.

Seattle SeaFair
Seattle, (206) 728-0123
This festival takes place during the last two weeks of July and the first week of August. It includes neighborhood parades, children's parades, a torch-light parade, the hydroplane races on Lake Washington, and more.

West Seattle Street Fair and Parade
Seattle, (206) 935-0904

August

Bubble Festival
Seattle, (206) 443-2001
The Pacific Science Center celebrates bubbles. The festival has entertainment and hands-on activities to show kids how bubbles are used in our everyday lives.

Hot Air Balloon Classic and Canterberry Fair
Kent, (206) 859-3991
The Hot Air Balloon Classic is a race of 35 colored balloons. There is also lots of family entertainment and food. Following the Balloon Classic, a medieval two-day festival called the Canterberry Fair features entertainers in medieval costumes, jousts, hands-on arts and crafts, food, and more.

KOMO Kidsfair
Seattle Center, (206) 684-7200

Evergreen State Fair
Monroe, (360) 794-7832

International Air Fair
Everett, (206) 355-2266

September

Bumbershoot
Seattle Center, (206) 622-5123
This arts festival, held Labor Day Weekend, includes big-name musicians, theater performances, art exhibits, and craft booths.

Festa Italiana
Seattle Center, (206) 684-7200
Celebrates Italian Seattle-ites.

Western Washington State Fair
Puyallup, (206) 841-5045

St. Demetrios Greek Festival
Seattle (206) 325-4347
Sample some tasty gyros!

Fiestas Patrias
Seattle Center, (206) 684-7200
Mexican and Latin American Independence are celebrated with dancing, entertainment, craft exhibits, and food.

October

Issaquah Salmon Days
Issaquah, (206) 392-0661
This weekend festival in Issaquah celebrates the salmon returning to Issaquah Creek. It features a parade, arts and crafts, and children's activities.

Molbak's Fairyland
Woodenville, (206) 483-5000
In its greenhouse, Molbak's Nursery creates a floral fairyland that shows scenes from children's favorite stories.

November

Festival of Light
Seattle Center, (206) 298-2521 or 441-1768
The Children's Museum celebrates winter holidays from around the world with music, storytelling, and hands-on activities.

Celebration Especially for Children
Bellevue, (206) 454-3322
This exhibit for kids is presented by the Bellevue Art Museum. It includes workshops and other special activities.

Model Railroad Show
Seattle Center, (206) 443-2001

Nordic Yulefest
Seattle, (206) 789-5707

December

Chanukah Celebration
Mercer Island, (206) 232-7115
The Stroum Jewish Community Center celebrates this Jewish holiday with games, lighting of menorahs, and food. Everyone is invited.

A Christmas Carol
Act Theatre, Seattle, (206) 285-5110

Gingerbread House Display
Sheridan Hotel, Seattle, (206) 621-9000

KING 5 Winterfest
Seattle Center, (206) 684-7200
This winter festival for kids continues from late November to early January. It features daily entertainment, ice skating, arts and crafts workshops, and more.

The Nutcracker
Pacific Northwest Ballet, Seattle, (206) 292-2787

Science Circus
Seattle, (206) 443-2001

Teddy Bear Suite
Four Seasons Hotel,
Seattle, (206) 621-1700

For more listings of events throughout the year check:
The Seattle Weekly
The Seattle Times, Thursday and Saturday editions
The Seattle PI, Friday edition

RESOURCE GUIDE: WHEN, WHAT, AND HOW MUCH?

Although all of the sites listed in this guide offer programs for children and families, not all programs offered by these places are suitable. Before attending a theater production, it is a good idea to have your parents check to see if the program offered at that time is OK for you to see.

The information contained in this Resource Guide changes often. Call before you plan your trip for current days and hours of operation as well as admission prices.

If You Get Lost

Do you know what to do if you get lost? Make a plan with your parents about what to do if you lose them. If you forget what to do and you're in a store, go to a person working at a cash register. If you are outside, look for a mother with children. Tell her you're lost.

If there is an emergency and you need the police, fire department, or an ambulance, you can dial 911 from any phone. You won't need coins.

Important Numbers

Injury, accident, or emergency 911
Seattle Police (206) 625-5011
Visitors Bureau, in Convention Center
(206) 461-5840
Washington Poison Center (206) 526-2121
Washington State Patrol (206) 455 7700
Should you get separated from your family, pick up a phone and call 911.

Transportation

Argosy Cruises, formerly called Harbor Tours
(206) 623-4252
Car Rentals:
  Avis (206) 448-1700
  Budget (206) 682-2277
  Hertz (206) 682-5050
Gray Line Airport Express (206) 626-6088
Gray Line Tours, bus (206) 626-5208
Metro Bus (206) 287-8463
Monorail, Westlake Center Station (206) 684-7200
Shuttle Express, to and from airport (800) 487-7433
Taxis:
  Farwest (206) 622-1717
  Graytop (206) 282-8222
  Yellow Cab (206) 622-6500
Victoria Clipper, boats to British Columbia
(206) 448-5000
Washington State Ferries,
Pier 50 (206) 464-6400
Waterfront Streetcar
(206) 553-3000

What They Cost and When They're Open

Al Young Bike Rentals, 3615 Northeast 45th, Seattle, 98105. Near start of Burke-Gilman Trail. (206) 524-2642

Alki Beach Park, Alki Avenue Southwest, Seattle. Park extends for 2 miles between Duwamish Head and the Lighthouse.

All for Kids Books and Music, 2900 Northeast Blakeley, Suite C, Seattle, 98105. Open Monday through Saturday 10 a.m. to 6 p.m., Sunday noon to 5 p.m. (206) 526-2768

Bhy Krake Park, Bigelow Avenue North and Comstock Place, Seattle.

Bill Speidel's Underground Tour, 610 First Avenue, Seattle, 98104. Daily tour times vary by season. Cost is $5.50 for adults, $4 for students ages 13 to 17, $2.50 for children ages 6 to 12. (206) 682-1511

Black Sun, in Volunteer Park.

Burke-Gilman Trail, begins at Gas Works Park, Seattle.

Center for Wooden Boats, 1077610 Valley Street, Seattle, 98109. Open daily Labor Day through June noon to 6 p.m., June through Labor Day 11 a.m. to 7 p.m. Admission to museum is free. Cost of boat rental is usually between $8 and $25 per hour. (206) 382-2628

Chinook's, Fisherman's Terminal, 1900 West Nickerson Street, Seattle, 98119. Open Monday through Thursday 11 a.m. to 11 p.m., Friday 11 a.m. to 11 p.m., Sunday 7:30 a.m. to 10 p.m. (206) 283-4665

City Kites-City Toys, Pike Place Market Hillclimb, Seattle. Open Sunday through Friday 11 a.m. to 5 p.m., Saturday 10 a.m. to 6 p.m. (206) 622-5349

Climb on a Rainbow Balloon Flights, call for locations and hours. Cost is $99 per person. Must be at least 5 years of age. (206) 364-0995

Columbia Seafirst Center, Columbia Street between Fourth and Fifth Avenues, Seattle. Observation deck hours Monday through Friday 8:30 a.m. to 4:30 p.m. Admission is $3.50 for adults, $1.75 for children. (206) 386-5151

Cucina! Cucina!, 901 Fairview Avenue, Seattle, 98109. Open daily 11:30 a.m. to 11 p.m. (206) 447-2782

Don Armeni Park Boat Ramp, Harbor Avenue Southwest, near California Avenue, Seattle. Admission is free.

Discovery Park and Daybreak Star Cultural Center, 36th Avenue West and West Government Way, Seattle, 98199. Park open daily dawn to dusk, Visitors Center open 8:30 a.m. to 5 p.m. Daybreak Star open Wednesday through Saturday 10 a.m. to 5 p.m. (206) 386-4236 and (206) 285-4425

Elliott Bay Books, 101 South Main Street, Seattle, 98104. Open Monday through Saturday 10 a.m. to 11 p.m., Sunday noon to 6 p.m. (206) 624-6600

F.A.O. Schwarz, 1420 Fifth Avenue, Seattle, 98101. Open Monday through Saturday 10 a.m. to 7 p.m., Sunday 11 a.m. to 6 p.m. (206) 442-9500

Fishing Pier 57, Waterfront at foot of University Street, Seattle. Open dawn to dusk. Admission is free to everyone.

Fishing Pier at Seacrest Park, 1660 Harbor Avenue Southwest, Seattle. Open dawn to dusk. Admission is free.

Fishing Pier at Seward Park, entrance on Lake Washington Boulevard near the foot of Orcas Street, Seattle. Restrooms. Open dawn to dusk. Admission is free.

Freeway Park, bounded by Sixth and Eighth Avenues, and University and Spring Streets, Seattle.

The Gap, Fourth Avenue and Pine Street, Seattle, 98101. Open Monday through Saturday 9:30 a.m. to 7:30 p.m., Sunday 11 a.m. to 6 p.m. (206) 625-1470

Garden Court at Four Seasons Olympic Hotel, 411 University Street, Seattle, 98101. Winnie the Pooh Brunch served Sundays 10 a.m. to 1:30 p.m. Call for information about Children's Tea. (206) 621-1700

Gas Works Park, on Lake Union, off North Northlake Way and Meridian, Seattle. Open daily. Admission is free.

Glass House Art, 311 Occidental Avenue South, Seattle, 98104. Open daily 10 a.m. to 5 p.m. No glass-blowing demonstrations 11:30 a.m to 12:30 p.m. (206) 682-9939

Golden Gardens Park, north end of Seaview Avenue Northwest and from Northwest 80th to Northwest 95th Street, Seattle.

Great Winds Kite Shop, 402 Occidental Avenue South, Seattle, 98104. Open daily 10 a.m. to 5:30 p.m. (206) 624-6886

Gregg's Greenlake Cycle

You can rent bikes at Gregg's Greenlake Cycle.

Gregg's Greenlake Cycle, 7007 Woodlawn Northeast, Seattle, 98115. Open Monday through Friday 9:30 a.m. to 9 p.m., Saturday and Sunday 9:30 a.m. to 6 p.m. Cost is $5 per hour. (206) 523-1822

Greenlake Boat Rentals, 7351 East Greenlake Drive North, Seattle, 98115. Open April through September 30. Cost is $8 to $12 per hour. (206) 527-0171

Greenlake Park, East Greenlake Drive North and West Greenlake Drive North, Seattle. Open daily. Admission is free.

Guido's Pizza, 7900 East Greenlake Drive North, Seattle, 98115. Open daily 11 a.m. to 10 p.m. (206) 522-5553

Hamilton Viewpoint, California Avenue Southwest and Southwest Donald Street, Seattle, 98116.

Highland Ice Arena, 18005 Aurora Avenue North, Seattle, 98133. Public sessions year-round. Admission is $4 for adults, $3.50 for kids ages 6 to 12, free for kids 5 and under. Skate rental is $2. Call for skating times. (206) 546-2431

Hiram M. Chittenden Locks, 3015 Northwest 54th Street, off Northwest Market Street and 32nd Avenue Northwest, Seattle. Visitors Center open daily 10 a.m. to 7 p.m. Guided tours daily at 1 p.m. and 3:30 p.m. Admission is free. (206) 783-7059

Iron Horse Restaurant, 311 Third Avenue South, Seattle. Open Sunday through Thursday 11 a.m. to 8 p.m., Friday and Saturday 11 a.m. to 9 p.m. (206) 223-9506

International Children's Park, Seventh Avenue South and South Lane Street, Seattle. Open daily. Admission is free.

Issaquah Fish Hatchery, 125 West Sunset Way, Issaquah. Open daily 8 a.m. to 4:30 p.m. Admission is free. (206) 392-3180

Ivar's Acres of Clams and Fish Bar, Pier 54, Waterfront, Seattle, 98101. Open daily Memorial Day through Labor Day 11 a.m. to 11 p.m., rest of the year 11 a.m. to 10 p.m. (206) 624-6852

Ivar's Salmon House, 401 Northlake Way, north side of Lake Union, Seattle, 98105. Lunch served Monday through Friday 11 a.m. to 2 p.m., dinner 4:30 p.m. to 11 p.m. Call for weekend hours. (206) 632-0767

Kerry Park Viewpoint, 211 West Highland Drive, Seattle. Open daily. Admission is free.

Key Arena, Seattle Center. Home of the Seattle SuperSonics. (206) 684-8582

Kingdome, 201 South King Street, Seattle. Home of the Mariners and Seahawks. Tours Monday through Saturday mid-April to mid-September. Cost is $4 for kids ages 12 and over, $2 for kids ages 11 and under. (206) 296-3128

Klondike Gold Rush National Historical Park, 117 South Main Street, Seattle. Open 9 a.m. to 5 p.m. Daily park ranger tour of Pioneer Square Historic District daily at 1:30 p.m. (206) 553-7220

Lincoln Park/Coleman Pool, Fauntleroy Southwest and Southwest Webster, Seattle. Park open daily. Admission is free. Coleman Pool open daily June through August noon to 7 p.m. Cost is $2.25 per session. (206) 684-7494

Magnuson Park and NOAA, Sand Point Way Northeast and 65th Northeast, Seattle, 98115. NOAA, 7600 Sand Point Way Northeast. Open daily 6:30 a.m. to dusk. Admission is free.

Market Café, Westin Hotel, 1900 Fifth Avenue, Seattle, 98101. Open daily 6 a.m. to 10 p.m. (206) 728-1000

Museum of Doll Art, 1116 108th Avenue Northeast, Bellevue, 98044. Open Monday through Thursday 10 a.m. to 5 p.m., Friday and Saturday 10 a.m. to 5 p.m., Sunday 1 p.m. to 5 p.m. Admission is $6 for adults, $4 for kids ages 5 to 17. (206) 455-1116

Museum of Flight, 9404 East Marginal Way South, Seattle, 98108. Open daily 10 a.m. to 5 p.m., Thursday 10 a.m. to 9 p.m. Admission is $6 for adults, $3 for kids ages 6 to 15. (206) 764-5720

Museum of History and Industry, 2700 24th Avenue East, at East Hamlin Street, Seattle, 98112. Open daily 10 a.m. to 5 p.m. Admission is $5.50 for kids ages 13 and over, $3 for kids ages 6 to 12, $1 for children ages 2 to 5. (206) 324-1125

Myrtle Edwards Park, Alaskan Way between West Bay and West Thomas, Seattle. Park begins just north of Pier 70.

Nike Town, Sixth Avenue and Pike Street, Seattle, 98101. Offers the latest in sports apparel and accessories.

Naramore Fountain, Sixth Avenue and Seneca Street, Seattle. One of downtown's most popular attractions.

Nordic Heritage Museum, 3014 Northwest 67th Street, Seattle, 98117. Open Tuesday through Saturday 10 a.m. to 4 p.m., Sunday noon to 4 p.m. Admission is $3 for adults, $2 for college students, $1 for kids ages 6 to 16, free for children 6 and under. (206) 789-5707

Northwest Trek, 11610 Trek Drive East, Eatonville, 98328. Open daily March through October 9:30 a.m. to dusk, Friday, Saturday, Sunday, and selected holidays the rest of the year. Call for guided tour schedule. Cost is $7.75 for adults, $5.75 for kids ages 5 to 17, $3.25 for children ages 3 to 4. (206) 832-6117 or (800) 433-8735

Occidental Park and Mall, between South Main and South Washington Streets, and on Occidental Avenue in Pioneer Square, Seattle.

Ocean City, 609 South Weller, Seattle, 98104. Open daily 9 a.m. to 3 p.m. (206) 623-2333

Olympic Game Farm, 1423 Ward Road, Sequim, 98382. Meet animal stars from movies and television. Open daily year-round 9 a.m. to dusk. Admission is $6 for adults, $5 for kids ages 5 to 12. (360) 683-4295 or (800) 778-4295

Omnidome, Pier 59, Seattle, 98101. Daily film program continuous from 10 a.m. Arrive 10 minutes early for each seating. Admission is $6 for adults, $5 for kids ages 13 to 18, $4 for kids ages 3 to 12. (206) 622-1868

Pacific Northwest Ballet, 301 Mercer Street, Seattle, 98109. Season runs September through June. Tickets range $11 to $62. (206) 441-9411 or 441-2424

Pacific Picnic, 1601 Fifth Avenue, Westlake Center, Seattle, 98101. Open Monday through Friday 9:30 a.m to 9 p.m., Saturday 9:30 a.m. to 7 p.m., Sunday 11 a.m. to 6 p.m. (206) 467-1600

Pacific Science Center/Carol Harrold

Play tic-tac-toe with a 10-foot tall robot in the Tech Zone at the Pacific Science Center.

Pacific Science Center, Seattle Center. Open daily mid-June through Labor Day 10 a.m. to 6 p.m., rest of the year and Saturday and Sunday 10 a.m to 5 p.m. Admission is $6.50 for adults, $5.50 for kids ages 8 to 13, $3.50 for kids ages 2 to 5. (206) 443-2880

Pike Place Market, at Pike Street and First Avenue, Seattle. Open Monday through Saturday 9 a.m. to 6 p.m., Sunday 11 a.m. to 5 p.m. Walking tours the last Saturday of each month, reservations required. (206) 682-7453

Pioneer Square, bounded by Alaskan Way and Second Avenue South, and Yesler Way and South King Street, Seattle.

Scandies, 2301 Northwest Market Street, Seattle, 98107. This is a popular Scandinavian restaurant in Northwest Seattle. Open Monday through Saturday 9 a.m. to 5 p.m., Sunday 8 a.m. to 3 p.m. (206) 783-5080

Seacrest Park and Boathouse, 1600 Harbor Avenue Southwest, Seattle, 98116. Open Wednesday through Sunday, July through October 4:30 a.m. to 8 p.m., November through June 5.30 a.m. to 5 p.m. Boat rentals cost $11 per hour, boats without motors cost $15 per day. Fishing pier is free. (206) 932-1050

SeaFair, Seattle. A festival celebrated during the last two weeks of July and first week of August. City-wide celebration. Most activities are free. Call for details. (206) 728-0123

Seattle Aquarium, Pier 59, off Alaskan Way, Seattle, 98101. Open daily Labor Day through Memorial Day 10 a.m. to 5 p.m., Memorial Day through Labor Day 10 a.m. to 7 p.m. Admission is $6 for adults, $4.50 for kids ages 6 to 18, $2.25 for children ages 3 to 5. (206) 386-4320

Seattle Art Museum, 100 University Street, Seattle, 98101. Open Tuesday through Sunday 10 a.m. to 5 p.m., Thursday 10 a.m. to 9 p.m. Admission is $6 for adults, free for kids ages 12 and under with an adult. (206) 654-3100

Seattle Asian Art Museum, 1400 East Prospect Street, in Volunteer Park, Seattle, 98122. Same hours and admission fees as Seattle Art Museum. (206) 654-3100

Seattle Center, bounded by First Avenue North and Fifth Avenue North, and Denny Way and Mercer Street, head for the Space Needle. Center House food concessions open daily Labor Day through Memorial Day 11 a.m to 6 p.m., Memorial Day through Labor Day 11 a.m. to 8 p.m. and Friday and Saturday 11 a.m. to 9 p.m. (206) 684-8582

Seattle Children's Museum, Seattle Center, Center House. Open Tuesday through Sunday 10 a.m. to 5 p.m. Admission is $3.50. (206) 298-2511

Seattle Children's Theatre, Charlotte Marlin Theatre, Seattle Center. Season runs October through May. Tickets are $14.50 for adults, $8.50 for kids. Call for performance schedules. (206) 441-3322

Seattle Mariners, Kingdome, 201 South King Street, Seattle. Baseball season runs April through September. Tickets are $5.50 to $12.50 for adults, $4 to $5 for kids. Be sure to call ahead of time. (206) 628-3555

Seattle SuperSonics, Key Arena, Seattle Center. Season runs September through May. Tickets range $7 to $42. (206) 281-5800

Seattle Thunderbirds, Key Arena, Seattle Center. Season runs September through March. Tickets range $7 to $10. (206) 448-7825

The Secret Garden Children's Bookshop

Poet Janet Wong autographs copies of her books at the Secret Garden Children's Bookshop.

Secret Garden Children's Bookshop, 6115 15th Avenue Northwest, Seattle, 98107. Open Monday through Saturday 10 a.m. to 6 p.m., Sunday 1 p.m. to 5 p.m. (206) 789-5006

Smith Tower, 506 Second Avenue, Seattle. Observation deck open Monday through Friday 9 a.m. to 11 a.m., 1:30 p.m to 4:30 p.m., 5:30 p.m to 10 p.m., Saturday and Sunday 9 a.m. to 10 p.m. Admission is $2 for adults, $1 for kids ages 12 and under, free for children under 6. (206) 682-9393

Southgate Roller Rink, 9646 17th Avenue Southwest, Seattle. Admission ranges $4 to $6 for two-hour sessions. Includes skate rental. Call for hours. (206) 762-4030

Space Needle, Seattle Center. Observation deck open daily 8 a.m. to midnight. Admission is $7 for adults, $3.50 for kids ages 5 to 12, free for children under 5. (206) 443-2111

Spud Fish and Chips, 2666 Alki Avenue Southwest, Seattle, 98116. Also located at 6860 East Greenlake Way North. Open daily 11 a.m. to 10 p.m. (206) 938-0606 and (206) 524-0565 respectively.

St. James Cathederal, 804 Ninth Avenue, Seattle. (206) 622-3559

Temple de Hirsch Sinai, East Pike Street and 16th Avenue, Seattle. (206) 323-8486

The Old Spaghetti Factory, 2801 Elliott Avenue, across from Pier 70, Seattle. Open Monday through Friday, lunch 11:30 to 2 p.m. and dinner 5 p.m. to 10 p.m., Saturday 5 p.m. to 11 p.m., Sunday noon to 10 p.m. (206) 441-7724

Thomas Burke Memorial Washington State Museum, Northeast 45th Street and 17th Avenue Northeast, on University of Washington campus, Seattle, 98195. Open daily 10 a.m. to 5 p.m., Thursday 10 a.m. to 9 p.m. Admission is free, but donations of $3 for adults, $1.50 for kids ages 6 to 18 are suggested. (206) 543-5590

Three Girls Bakery, Sanitary Market Building, Pike Place Market, Seattle. Open Monday through Saturday 7 a.m. to 6 p.m. (206) 622-1045

Tillicum Village, Blake Island. Tickets include boat, dinner, and entertainment. Prices are $54 for adults, $35 for teens ages 13 to 19, $21 for kids ages 6 to 12, $10 for children 4 to 5, free for children under 4. Call for schedule. (206) 443-1244

Trinity Episcopal Church, Eighth Avenue and James Street, Seattle. (206) 624-5337

University of Washington Huskies, University of Washington campus, Husky Stadium on Montlake Boulevard Northeast, Seattle, 98115. Season runs September through November. Tickets range $12 to $26. (206) 543-2000

University of Washington Observatory, on campus, 17th Avenue Northeast and 45th Street, Seattle, 98195. Kids must be with parents. Open Monday, Wednesday, and Thursday 9 p.m. to 11 p.m. Admission is free. (206) 543-0126

Mary Levin/University of Washington

This skeleton of a giant ice-age ground sloth can be found at the Thomas Burke Museum.

University of Washington Waterfront Activity Center, on campus, behind Husky Stadium, Seattle. Open Monday through Friday 10 a.m. to dusk, Saturday and Sunday 9 a.m. to dusk. Boat rentals cost $4 per hour. (206) 543-9433

Uwajimaya, 519 Sixth Avenue South, Seattle, 98104. Open daily 9 a.m. to 8 p.m., in the summer until 9 p.m. (206) 624-6248

Velodrome Bike Racing, Marymoor Park, Redmond. Season runs May through September. Tickets cost $3. Call ahead of time for special events. (206) 389-5825

Vertebrae, 1001 Fourth Avenue, Building Plaza, Seattle.

Viewland-Hoffman Electrical Substation, North 105th Street and Freemont Avenue, Seattle.

Volunteer Park, 15th Avenue and East Galer Street, Seattle. (206) 625-8901

Waiting for the Interurban, Freemont Avenue North and North 34th Street, Seattle.

Washington Park Arboretum Waterfront Trails, 2700 24th Avenue East, Seattle. Start at Museum of History and Industry parking lot.

Waterfall Park, Main Street at Second Avenue South, Seattle. Open daily, in winter 8 a.m. to 4 p.m, in summer 8 a.m. to 6 p.m. Admission is free. (206) 624-6096

Westlake Center, Pine Street between Fourth and Fifth Avenues, Seattle. Open Monday through Friday 9:30 a.m. to 8 p.m., Saturday 9:30 a.m. to 7 p.m., Sunday 11 a.m. to 6 p.m. (206) 467-1600

Wild Waves and Enchanted Village, 36201 Enchanted Parkway South, Federal Way, 98003. Open mid-April through Labor Day. Call for hours. Admission to Enchanted Village only ranges $9 to $11. Admission to both Enchanted Village and Wild Waves ranges $16 to $18.50. (206) 661-8000

Wing Luke Asian Museum, 407 Seventh Avenue South, Seattle. Open Tuesday through Friday 11 a.m. to 4:30 p.m., Saturday and Sunday noon to 4 p.m. Admission is $2.50 for adults, $1.50 for students and kids 12 and up, 75 cents for children ages 6 to 11. (206) 623-5124

Woodland Park Zoo, 5500 Phinney Avenue North, Seattle, 98103. Open weekdays April through September 9:30 a.m. to 6 p.m., October through March 9:30 a.m. to 5 p.m., weekends and holidays opens at 8:30 a.m. Admission is $7 for adults, $5.25 for college students, $4.50 for kids ages 6 to 17, $2.25 for children ages 3 to 5, free for children under 2. (206) 684-4800

Ye Olde Curiosity Shop and Museum, 1001 Alaskan Way, Pier 54, Seattle, 98104. Open Monday through Thursday 9:30 a.m to 6 p.m., extended summer hours. (206) 682-5844

ANSWERS TO PUZZLES

page 11

page 13

page 19

K O N A T K M E S O P M Y P V U H
H P H F R D Q S Y M H E B A O N H
N Y N L S G A I N N P T S B L T F
T T P O D R S K A T I N G U L U D
R A T W G M N R D V C E N T E D N
E E U E M D F N G N N O G T Y E Y
E D S R G U N N H U I U Y E B W R
S A X S P C I N D K C L M R A D W
P O N D U K R O W B O A T F L Q T
U I S E I S U R N P Y D N L L U B
R O T B L K I T E U L I M Y N F S
D Y D N I O P Y F R I S B E E Q R

page 21

page 23

page 25

page 27

			1B	A	L	L		
2P	O	L	E					
			N					
	3P	I	C	N	I	4C		
	A		H			A		
	R					M		
	5K	I	6T	E		E		
			R			R		
7B	I	K	E		8W	A	L	K
			E					
			S					

page 29

page 37

page 39

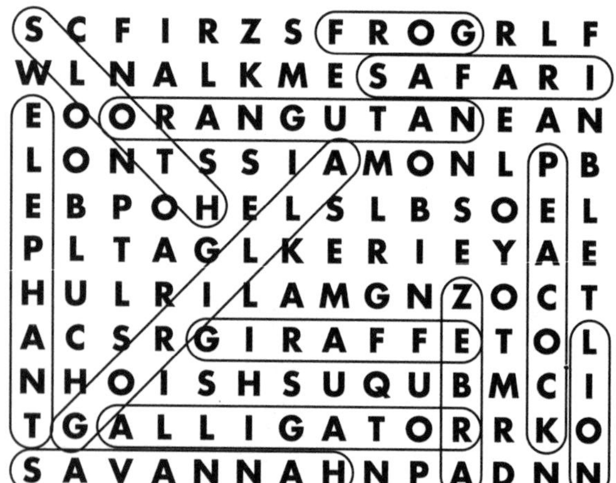

page 43

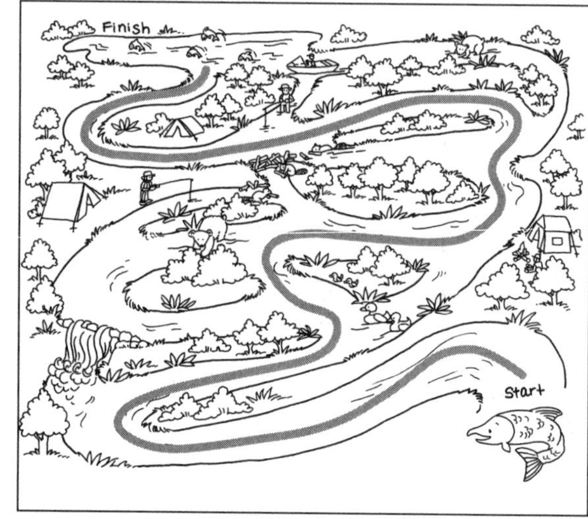

page 45

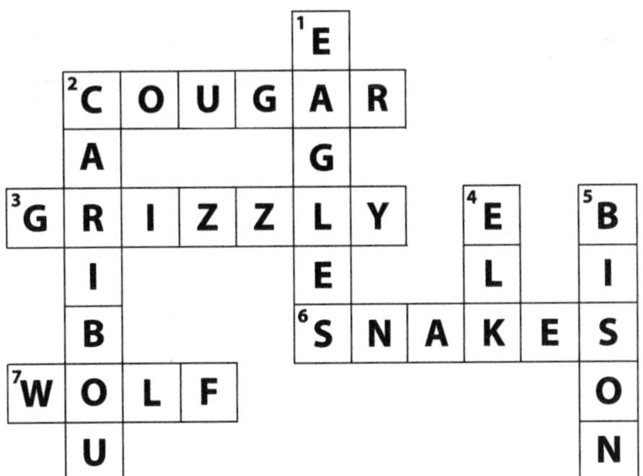

page 51

page 53

page 57

page 65

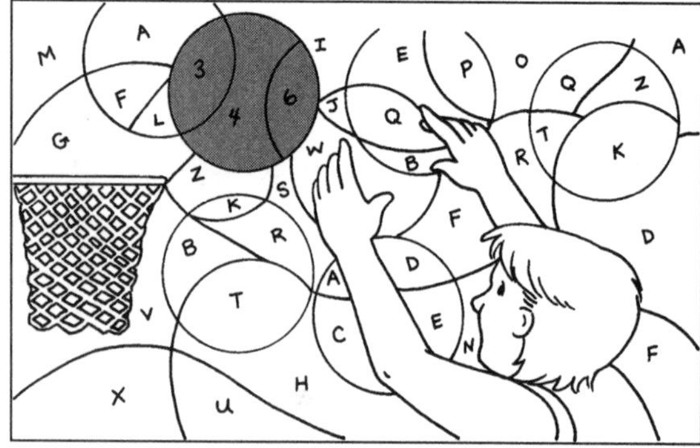

Answer: a basketball

page 67

page 69

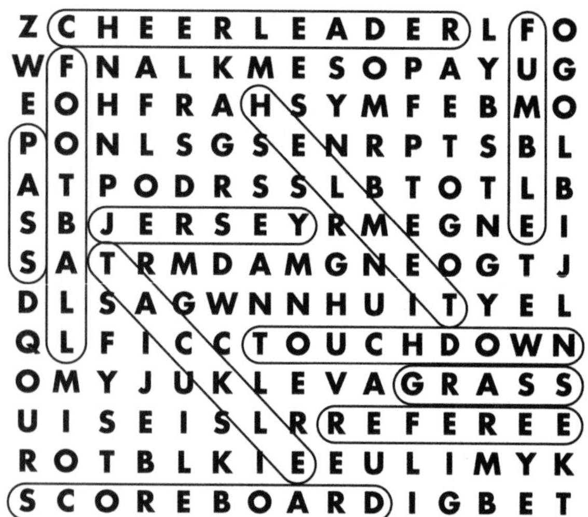

page 75

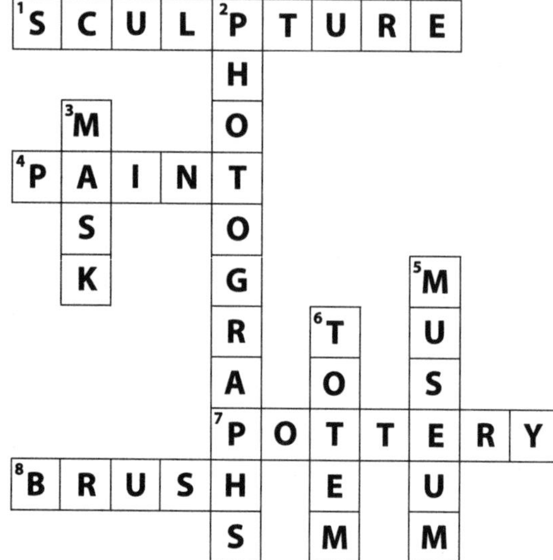

page 79

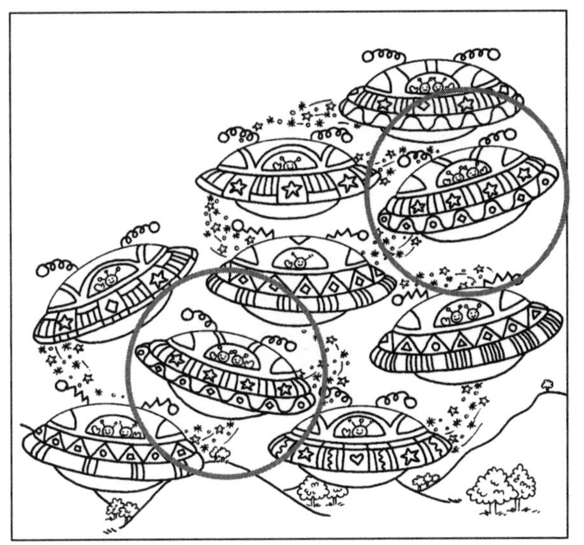

page 83

page 85

page 95

page 97

page 99

page 101

Z C F O R E S T A D E R L F D
W F N A L K F O O D P A Y N A
E O H F R A H S Y M F E A M N
P O N L S S A L M O N L S B C
A B P O M E S S L B S O T L I
S E T A G A K E R I E Y N E N
S A L R M L A M G N E O G T G
D C S A G T N N H U I T Y E L
Q H F I S H S U Q U A M I S H
O M Y J O K L E V A C R I T S
U I S E N S L R N P Y D N L C
R O T B G K I E E U L I M Y K
S C T E S B E A P A R K B E T

page 107

page 109

page 111

GEOGRAPHICAL INDEX: WHERE IS EVERYTHING?

Capital Hill and First Hill

St. James Cathedral
Seattle Asian Art Museum
Temple de Hirsch Sinai
Trinity Episcopal Church
Volunteer Park

Downtown

F.A.O. Schwarz
Freeway Park
Four Seasons Olympic Hotel
The Gap
Monorail Terminal
Nike Town
Naramore Fountain
Pike Place Market
Seattle Art Museum
Vertebrae
Westin Hotel
Westlake Center

International District

International Children's Park
Ocean City
Uwajimaya
Wing Luke Museum

Lake Union and Fremont

Al Young Bike Rentals
Burke-Gilman Trail
Center for Wooden Boats
Cucina! Cucina!
Gas Works Park
Ivar's Salmon House
Waiting for the Interurban

North and Northwest Seattle

Greenlake Park
Guido's Pizza
Highland Ice Arena
Hiram M. Chittenden Locks
Nordic Heritage Museum
Scandies
Viewland-Hoffman Substation
Woodland Park Zoo

Northeast Seattle

Husky Stadium
Magnuson Park/NOAA
Museum of History and Industry
Sound Garden
Thomas Burke Memorial Museum
University of Washington
Washington Park Arboretum
Waterfront Trails

Pioneer Square

Bill Speidel's Underground Tour
Columbia Seafirst Center

Elliott Bay Books
Glass House Art
Great Winds Kite Shop
Klondike Gold Rush Museum
The Kingdome
Occidental Mall and Park
Smith Tower
Waterfall Park

Queen Anne Hill and Magnolia

Bhy Krake Park
Chinook's
Daybreak Star Cultural Center
Discovery Park
Fisherman's Terminal
Kerry Park

Seattle Center

Fun Forest Amusement Park
Key Arena
Monorail Terminal
Pacific Northwest Ballet
Pacific Science Center
Seattle Children's Museum
Seattle Children's Theatre
Seattle Fudge
Space Needle

South Seattle

Fishing Pier at Seward Park
Museum of Flight
Seward Park
Southgate Roller Rink

Waterfront

Ferry Terminal
Fishing Pier 57
Ivar's Acres of Clams
Myrtle Edwards Park
The Old Spaghetti Factory
Omnidome
Seattle Aquarium
Waterfront Streetcar
Ye Olde Curiosity Shop

West Seattle

Alki Beach Park
Boat House at Seacrest Park
Coleman Pool at Lincoln Park
Don Armeni Park Boat Ramp
Fishing Pier, Seacrest Park
Hamilton Viewpoint
Lincoln Park/Coleman Pool
Luna Park Café
Seacrest Park/Boat House
Spud Fish and Chips

Out of Town

Climb on a Rainbow Balloon Flights
Enchanted Village/Wild Waves
Issaquah Fish Hatchery
Museum of Doll Art
Northwest Trek
Olympic Game Farm
Tillicum Village
Velodrome Bike Racing
Wild Waves/Enchanted Village

INDEX